A RESIDENTIAL HOTEL

Five minutes walk from Broadway
2 Blocks to Public Library Theater District

CROWN HOTEL

BARNEY H. NEMO, Mgr.

Private Baths, Steam Heat, Switchboard
Ground Floor Lobby, Electric Elevator
Very Reasonable Transient and Weekly Rates

702 W. THIRD ST.
Los Angeles, Calif.

Telephone
MUtual 2255

Roosevelt Apartments

334 South Figueroa Street
Los Angeles, Cal.
Sunset Main 5041 : : : : Home 3404

From $14.00 a Month up.

Three Rooms Furnished Complete. Large Sitting Room, Kitchen, Hot Water, Gas Range, Alcove Bedroom, Porcelain Bath, Telephone. : : : :

New. Elegant. Close in.

T. WIESENDANGER, Proprietor

LOS ANGELES
Hotel Trenton
427 S. OLIVE ST.

APARTMENT HOTEL
The ENGSTRUM
623 W - FIFTH

New NORTHERN HOTEL

420 W. 2ND ST., NEAR HILL ST.
LOS ANGELES, CALIFORNIA

Parlor and Lobby of Hotel Trenton, 427 South Olive St., Los Angeles, Cal.

Cumberland Hotel

HOTEL AND APARTMENTS
243 SOUTH OLIVE STREET

BUNKER HILL
LOS ANGELES

BUNKER HILL LOS ANGELES
ESSENCE OF SUNSHINE AND NOIR

NATHAN MARSAK

BUNKER HILL, LOS ANGELES
Essence of Sunshine and Noir
By Nathan Marsak

Copyright © 2020 Nathan Marsak

Design by J. Eric Lynxwiler
Cover design by Amy Inouye, Future Studio

10 9 8 7 6 5 4 3 2

ISBN-13 978-1-62640-067-2 (print edition)

All rights reserved. No part of this book may be reproduced or transmitted in any form or by any means, electronic or mechanical, including photocopying, recording, or by an information storage and retrieval system, without express written permission from the publisher.

"Angel City Press" and the ACP logo are registered trademarks of Angel City Press. The names and trademarks of products mentioned in this book are the property of their registered owners.

Library of Congress Cataloging-in-Publication Data is available.

Published by Angel City Press, www.angelcitypress.com

Printed in Canada

▲ **First Street, looking west toward Grand Avenue from near Olive Street. Circa 1952.**

▶ **Three gents take in the day on the benches above the Hill Street tunnels. Circa 1954.**

Overleaf: An aerial view, looking north over the rooftops of Bunker Hill. Circa 1912.

CONTENTS

Foreword by Gordon Pattison — 8
Preface — 10

THE HISTORY OF BUNKER HILL

Beaudry's Beginnings — 14
Architecture of the Boom Years — 20
Transportation on the Hill — 25
Building Resumes: Beaux-Arts Comes to the Hill — 30
Mission Revival on the Hill — 33
Life on the Hill — 34
Hill Street — 45
An Early History of Redevelopment — 48
The Hill Casts a Long Shadow: Bunker Hill and Los Angeles Noir — 54
Redevelopment Takes Hold — 61
The 1960s: Demolition and Rebirth — 68

BUNKER HILL, LOS ANGELES

The Early Years — 76
The Boom of the Eighties — 84
The Apartment Age — 98
Life on the Hill — 108
Bunker Hill Noir — 120
Hill Street — 126
Fort Moore Hill — 136
Motive Power — 140
The Modern Age — 146
Early Demolition — 154
The CRA Years — 158
A New Era — 164

Afterword — 173
Image Credits — 174
Acknowledgments — 175
Location Index — 176

◀ An early-morning outing at the southeast corner of First and Olive Streets. 1953.

▶ Fifth Street, on Bunker Hill's southern border, served as a demarcation between the business district of downtown and residential Bunker Hill above. Stairs led from Fifth Street up to Hope Street through the 1930 retaining wall, which Carleton Winslow designed to complement the new Central Library across the street. November 1948.

FOREWORD

Welcome, time travelers. Come with my friend Nathan Marsak and me on a visit to Bunker Hill and its vanished nineteenth century neighborhood. The Los Angeles we live in today is an imposter. Whereas many older American cities have managed to keep at least some of their nineteenth century character, Los Angeles has not. This imposter stole Los Angeles's nineteenth century identity. The Los Angeles I was born into years ago was far different from the one we live in today because much that had been built in those days was still here when I was young.

I have been called a native son of Los Angeles's Bunker Hill, which, I am proud to say, is true. My earliest childhood memories are of the old Bunker Hill, the one that existed before redevelopment erased it in the 1960s. Now, fifty years after it was demolished, I might be one of the few people left in Los Angeles who not only remembers the old Bunker Hill, but actually lived up there, and whose family owned property on it. My father's family moved to Los Angeles from Indiana in 1932 in the depths of the Great Depression. They settled on Bunker Hill because it was conveniently adjacent to downtown and because it was affordable. By then, what had originally been the home of the city's affluent had become home to low-income families, artists, writers, elderly pensioners, and first-generation immigrants. They populated its old Victorians, which had become rooming houses and the other small hotels and apartments that covered the Hill. My grandmother soon found a job at Bullock's Department Store downtown. Like her neighbors, she commuted to work on Angels Flight, or maybe, because it was the Depression, she saved the nickel fare and walked. In fact, nearly all your needs could be met within walking distance when you lived on Bunker Hill. If you needed to go farther, you simply went to the foot of the Hill and boarded a Pacific Electric Red Car or one of the other streetcars which ran there.

In addition to working at Bullock's, my grandmother became landlady to several rooming houses on Bunker Hill. She worked hard, saved her money, and by 1937 she had enough to make down payments on two lovely old Victorian buildings up on South Bunker Hill Avenue. One was the Castle, about which you will learn more in this book, and the second was the house next door. The Victorians gave Bunker Hill its charm. Every building was different, all with intersecting angles, curved verandas, and turrets, domes, carved details, light, and shadows. And they all had names like the Chaspeak, the Rose, the Brousseau, the Brunson, the Melrose, the Salt Box, and the Castle.

In those days, the Hill's residents were by and large a mix of white, Asian, and Hispanic people. They lived quiet lives, sent their children to local schools, attended church, and shopped downtown or in the neighborhood stores on and

Gordon Pattison, on the sidewalk in front of 333 South Bunker Hill Ave., with the Castle in the background. 1947.

around the Hill. They bought their groceries at the Budget Basket Market, had their prescriptions filled at the Angels Flight Pharmacy, bought their deli items at the Nugent Delicatessen, had their shoes repaired and their laundry done all in the little commercial area on Third Street between Grand Avenue and Olive Street.

When World War II came, my father and many of his friends from the Hill went off to serve their country. When he came back, he brought with him his new wife, who is my mother, and me. Sadly, my grandmother had died while he was away, which meant he inherited the properties. The War hadn't changed the Hill much. It was still a quiet, mature neighborhood with well-tended yards where the soft sound of pigeons cooing, or the breeze rustling the palm trees, was occasionally interrupted by the sound of a distant siren coming up from the city down below. It was a time when men dressed in suits and hats, and women wore dresses and high heels every day. There were still a few cars with running boards. Even today, I still sometimes call a refrigerator an "icebox" because we had a wooden one and had ice delivered weekly to keep things cold inside.

Changes were coming, however. I have said that Bunker Hill's problem was one of geography. It was simply too close to City Hall. I can just imagine the city fathers sitting up there looking out the window and saying, "We have to get rid of all those old buildings." Los Angeles experienced a postwar population and building boom. In those days, Bunker Hill was described as a blighted slum which needed to be razed, populated by a constituency which was easy to overlook, low-income and elderly residents who needed to be removed. It was a majority-white neighborhood, albeit with a significant minority population. Economic exploitation can be colorblind. You just have to be powerless, unwanted, and unvalued to be exploited.

It started in the late 1940s with the building of the Hollywood Freeway on the north end and the Harbor Freeway on the west, followed by the clearing of the land where the Department of Water and Power, Music Center, and courthouse are now. The 4th Street cut isolated it on the south. However, much of the Old Bunker Hill between Hope and Hill Streets survived through the 1950s and into the 1960s when the Community Redevelopment Agency finally razed and eventually replaced it with what is there now. What happened to Bunker Hill is a story which needs to be told.

Come with us, time travelers, as Nathan Marsak peels away this modern overlay to reveal the old Bunker Hill and the old Los Angeles. There is none more qualified than Nathan to tell this story. As an architectural and Los Angeles historian, no one knows more about Bunker Hill. Walk with us on Bunker Hill's historic streets and see Angels Flight. Together we will find the Bunker Hill that was a mature, quiet urban neighborhood with well-tended yards. It was not the "blighted slum" that propaganda of the time said it was. Instead, it was a tranquil oasis above the busy city down below. If I still lived in the Castle, I'd invite you in. But I don't live there anymore. In fact, none of us who once made up this neighborhood community lives there now—Old Bunker Hill was ripped from the heart of Los Angeles fifty years ago. Before too many more years, it will pass from Los Angeles's living memory. But Old Bunker Hill isn't really gone. Instead, it floats ethereally in memory and in our hearts above Hope and Grand, Olive and Hill. It had a quiet dignity and timelessness that I miss.

Gordon Pattison, Los Angeles, 2019

PREFACE

I grew up in a big old house. My parents were less interested in its upkeep than they were in their books or their travels, so the big old house fell into gracious disrepair.

We lived in an area of our Santa Barbara suburb called the Hedgerow. Homes hid behind hedges, garnering all the more mystery about them. I developed an affection for mysterious old houses—ours especially, for while Santa Barbara is known for its bungalows and Spanish Colonial Revival architecture, ours was a bit of a white elephant. It was a big piece of foursquare Edwardiana, all tall Doric columns and multiple gables. The paint peeled, the grounds were overgrown—and I loved it.

While we didn't live in Los Angeles, we tuned in its television stations, so the city informed my youth, replete as it was with commercials for Pete Ellis Dodge and Colton Piano. Los Angeles felt like my backyard. I watched a lot of television. My favorite was *The Munsters*, on weekend reruns on KTLA. *The Munsters* taught me a lot. They were a loving, functional family in that grand gabled behemoth on Mockingbird Lane. And while I was—and am—enamored of the Addams Family, the Munsters were uniquely, particularly L.A. They were into hot rod culture, hung out with the Standells, and had a surf-music theme song. Herman Munster even tried out for the Dodgers. But, most saliently, they and their house represented not just the marginalized (heaven forfend a family of another color—in this case, green—move into one's neighborhood) but the trappings of blight: in one episode, wreckers buy the Munster's Queen Anne manse to demolish it for a parking lot. The Munster clan repels the invaders and saves the family's Victorian home. I would discover that it didn't always go so well for Victorian homes down in Los Angeles.

For my first trip to Los Angeles, a friend's family took me to meet Groucho Marx at his final public appearance in January 1977. There at the Wilshire Hyatt House I met my idol, and afterward my pal and I had lunch inside the hat at the Brown Derby. Very soon after, Groucho was dead; when I returned a few years later to the Derby, it had been demolished for a parking lot.

I have found that among academics, historians especially, there are usually formative moments of loss like these. That—or such traumatic experiences—breeds historians. Either way, on moving to Los Angeles in 1993 after graduate work in architectural history, I became enraptured with Bunker Hill, especially after watching *Kiss Me Deadly* and *Criss Cross* in the revival houses. I spent endless hours bending ears and elbows with barroom historians.

While circumstance propelled me to study the vanished built environment, I met folks from all walks of life who were similarly absorbed by Bunker Hill for any number of reasons—it was the tale of David vs Goliath, after all. Some people loved old L.A., and some were interested in the Hill's modern towers. Many were intrigued by its *noir* element. Mostly, there was a pronounced romance for this lost world, where somewhere in our collective memory there existed a grand patriciate, and their *haute monde*, fallen to cinematic ruin and expunged by progress, effaced without regard to how we, fifty years on, might wonder after the past.

And so I began this book. All that wondering has resulted in a lot of researching and collecting, which helped flesh out the tale of Bunker Hill, a tale that took twists and turns I could not have expected. I'm honored to be among the many to tell her story; I hope, at least, for this account to be the most complete and accurate. At the very least it's been a thrill to compile—and so I lay at your feet, for your edification and delectation, *Bunker Hill, Los Angeles*.

The Melrose Hotel (Joseph Cather Newsom, 1889) on South Grand Avenue under demolition. City Hall, four blocks east, keeps a watchful eye. 1957.

THE HISTORY OF BUNKER HILL

From left: Rose Mansion, with domed cupola; Brunson Mansion, with pointed tower; at far right, Crocker Mansion. The spire between the Rose and Brunson is an early 150-foot carbon arc lamp, a streetlight said to resemble the light of the full moon. At bottom center, the prominent building is Fort Street Methodist Episcopal Church. The Castle, on Bunker Hill Avenue, is to the left of the church's spire. Circa 1895.

Beaudry's Beginnings

Our story begins with a hill, a dusty promontory to the west of a river. This was the river that Spanish explorer Captain Fernando Javier Rivera y Moncada and his expeditionary force—the first overland party to reach California—saw in August 1769. Rivera's diarist, Father Juan Crespí, described the scene as "a very spacious valley, well grown with cottonwoods and sycamores, among which ran a beautiful river." No mention was made of the hill, but the river was named Nuestra Señora de los Ángeles de la Porciúncula.

Captain Rivera returned with a contingent of *pobladores*—forty-four settlers and a small contingent of soldiers—to settle a pueblo on the low hillside above the west bank of the river in the summer of 1781. The hill loomed above them; as the pueblo grew, it acted as a barrier against the yowling hinterland to the west. That was the hill's sole use; even the native Tongva people who had settled the area millennia ago had little use for it.

The promontory loomed over the growing pueblo, known to the Spaniards as Reiña de Los Angeles. On occasion, sheep would graze on the hill's grasses after the rains. In March 1825, Mexico overthrew Spanish rule, and the Mexican flag flew over Los Angeles until July 4, 1847, when Fort Moore was dedicated on the hill overlooking the Plaza.

Newly a part of the United States, Los Angeles was a difficult place in the 1850s and 1860s. It was populated by reprobates wandering south from the Sierra Nevada goldfields, earning it the nickname "Hell Town." It was rough, lawless. The little city of four thousand people was nearly abandoned after a disastrous cycle of drought, flooding, and the subsequent destruction of the cattle industry. After the drought of 1862–1865, many landowners like the Pico brothers and Lugo family had trouble paying taxes and servicing debt. As they began to lose property to foreclosure, a new word crept into the Los Angeles lexicon: subdivision. Former governor John J. Downey bought up most of the major land holdings along the river and split it up into small farming plots in 1865. In 1869, recent Ohio transplant Robert Maclay Widney engineered the purchase of 180,000 acres of Abel Stearns's extensive ranchos, which stretched from Long Beach into what is now Orange County, and created enormous subdivisions. Widney—who would come to live on the hill—began publishing the *Los Angeles Real Estate*

Looking south on Fort Street (later Broadway). Bunker Hill, at right, looms over the burgeoning city. 1869.

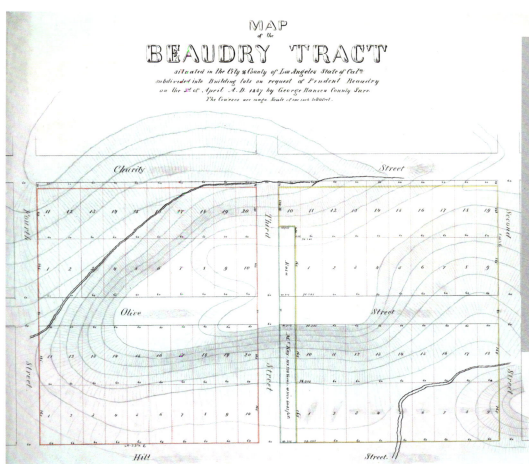

Prudent Beaudry: mayor, builder, visionary, Angeleno.

◀ Beaudry's initial purchase, surveyed and subdivided. 1867.

Advertiser in 1870, selling lots to families from Eastern states, mostly disenfranchised folk from the war-torn Confederate South. In 1869 Phineas Banning, an entrepreneur known as the "Father of the Port of Los Angeles," opened his railroad between Los Angeles and the port at San Pedro; this made the importation of building material cheaper and easier.

Los Angeles has always had men of visionary acumen, and one of particular importance made his mark around the same time: Prudent Beaudry. Beaudry was born in 1816 to a fine Québécois family, one of five brothers and three sisters. He won and lost numerous fortunes in mercantile ventures, including in the ice business, the syrup business, and in the shipping and commission game across Canada, Europe, New York, New Orleans, and many a point in between. After a disastrous warehouse fire in San Francisco, he elected to begin anew, as so many do, in Los Angeles. The year was 1852. Beaudry began to buy and sell office blocks; before long he was a wealthy and respected citizen of Los Angeles.

The story of Bunker Hill begins in earnest in March 1867, when Beaudry attended a public auction to purchase Jesse D. Hunter's property, twenty acres of steep hillside land roughly bounded by Fourth, Second, Charity, and Hill Streets, a plot that cost Beaudry $517. (Charity Street would be renamed Grand Avenue in February 1887.) After making this purchase, Beaudry angled to have the

Essence of Sunshine and Noir

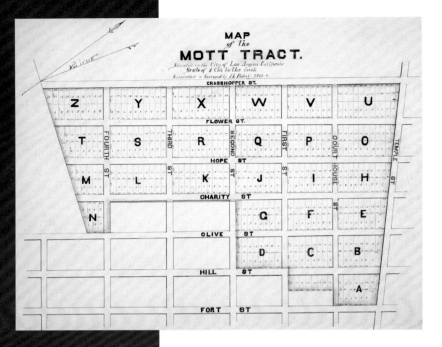

Stephen Mott's subdivision imposed order over Bunker Hill. 1868.

Common Council (which became the Los Angeles City Council in 1889) put the surrounding area up for sale. The Common Council's survey map, known as the Ord Survey, was drawn in 1849 and did not include the hill area to the west; Beaudry hired a surveyor, George Hansen, to draw a new map.

On Lt. Ord's 1849 map, the streets surrounding the hill simply ended, and Beaudry's new map elongated Calle de las Chapules (later known as Grasshopper Street, then Pearl, now Figueroa) on the west, Temple Street on the north, Hill Street on the east, and his lands on the south, up and over the hill. Hansen made the same map for land speculator Stephen H. Mott, and Mott acquired the remainder of the land; it became known as the Mott Tract. Hansen received a number of lots as payment.

There has long been a question as to how Bunker Hill was named. Some say it was for the centennial anniversary of the famous Revolutionary War battle; others contest that it was in reference to those bunkers (strictly speaking, not bunkers but a breastwork fortification) dug into the northernmost point of the hill in 1847 by the Mormon Battalion. An article in the *Los Angeles Herald* from December 16, 1873 details its naming, and indicates that a bit of both came into play:

> A little over a year more, and the 100th anniversary of the Battle of Bunker Hill will take place. A little band of heroes, then inaugurated a struggle, which brought untold results. It is very fitting that their deeds should be commemorated. The nation at large is very justly arranging for a celebration on an extensive scale, of the centennial anniversary of this event. This will instill patriotic impulse into the souls of those of the coming generations, and prepares them for the struggles, which they, in life, must undergo. Overhanging Los Angeles is a hill similar to Bunker Hill—nay, it is larger. From it all the city can be seen and the country for miles around. On this hill also, are military marks, the remnants of a fort, which was built for the protection of liberty in this State. This hill has an avenue running along its crest, and our friend Beaudry, through whose influence chiefly it has been opened, has very appropriately named it Bunker Hill avenue.

With Bunker Hill Avenue crowning the hill after 1873, it has been generally surmised that the general geographic region took on the name "Bunker Hill" about this time or soon after. However, an investigation of newspaper accounts reveals that through the remainder of the century, the area was generally referred to as "the western hills," and "the hill section" or "hill district," and property owners often designated as "hill dwellers." The first known use of "Bunker Hill" as a term directly relating to the area as a whole occurs on June 28th, 1900, when a short note in the *Los Angeles Times* read

> Bunker Hill Engine-House: At the last session of the Council, the petition of J. Brousseau et al. for better fire-fighting facilities in the Bunker Hill district was referred to the Fire Commission. The petition represents that on Hill, Olive and Hope streets, and on Grand

and Bunker Hill avenues, where they pass through the district, there is insufficient protection from fires. Owing to the elevated ground the fire engines experience great difficulty in getting quickly to the fires.

(For the record, Bunker Hill resident Julius Brousseau had his petition eventually granted, and the Dennis & Farwell-designed Engine Company No. 16 was built at 139 North Hope St. in 1904.)

Beaudry's first challenge in developing his newly subdivided lots was getting water up to the hill. Getting water anywhere in Los Angeles had been a challenge: the *Zanja Madre*, or Mother Ditch, was an open trench that worked well enough as the pueblo grew out of its infancy, but the water was subject to contamination. Dryden & Marchesseault's 1857 closed-pipe system of auger-bored pine logs quickly rotted out; Sainsevain's 1860s system of iron pipes washed away. Beaudry devised his own plan to divert water from the Los Angeles River into ravines where it could be pumped into the subdivision, and in 1867 he formed the Canal and Reservoir Company. In 1868, the Common Council awarded a city waterworks project to Beaudry and his outfit, which reincorporated as the Los Angeles City Water Company. Beaudry set to work on a huge reservoir and pump system that supplied water to the hill from the river and marshy lowlands. By 1869 he had built two reservoirs 240 feet deep, laid eleven miles of iron pipe, and drove forty thousand gallons of water an hour to his hillside properties with a steam-driven pump.

The following article from the *Los Angeles Herald* of December 13, 1873, sums up the activity:

> Yesterday, in company with Prudent Beaudry, we had the opportunity of riding over the hills to the north of the city, and were quite surprised to see the progress made by the city in that direction. It is so easy to accomplish what has been accomplished, and this is so much;
>
> Streets are being opened in all directions. Temple Street, Third Street and Fourth Street are being graded, and Bunker Hill avenue is run parallel to Spring and Fort, along the crest of the hill.
>
> It has always been considered impossible to get water on these hills, but with little labor, and at a comparatively light expense, our friend Beaudry has brought this around, and now he is laying pipes all over the hills in a most prodigal way. Long lines of ditches, and piles of pipe are everywhere, and the holes are already dug for pepperell and gum trees soon to speckle the hill top and sides.
>
> The tank which waters the hillsides holds 3,000 gallons and ought to keep the people and land well watered, but this is not enough for Mr. Beaudry. He proposes to erect still other tanks, and put in an engine to fill them. The supply of water is inexhaustible, and now is put "where it will do the most good."
>
> The view from the hill is most beautiful. Why people will dwell in the valley when they can live on the hilltop is more than a reasoning man can see. Yesterday the snow capped mountains in the distance were glinting and glittering in the pure sun light and looked as though nature, showing her joy that the rain had come and was gone, was saying in her own way and in the clearest tones, "God is good, the harvest will be abundant." The city lay at our feet with its green and leopard-colored orange groves, its long lines of pepperell and its rippling willow-lined zanjas. The river stretched along and could be traced by the willows which grow on its banks. In the points of the compass the country could be seen for miles upon miles away. One could scarcely help being romantic and poetical if they lived up the hill.

The reporter describes how Beaudry surveyed and platted all the lots, and wrote that they were available for inspection and sale at reasonable terms—fifteen dollars down, fifteen dollars per month, no interest, immediate possession; lots were priced from $100 to $525. Street grading was a mammoth undertaking, but Hill, Olive, Flower, and Hope Streets were completed in 1874. Beaudry was elected mayor of Los Angeles in December of that year.

While early photographs suggest that there were already small structures at the base of the Hill at the time of Beaudry's development—most likely buildings ancillary to sheep grazing—the first recorded structure on the Hill was the African Methodist Episcopal Church, at the corner of Fourth and Charity Streets, in 1869; its bishop was T.M.D. Ward. Others would soon follow up onto the arcadian acreage.

Just as structures began to dot Bunker Hill, 1875 arrived: it was a tough year for Los Angeles. The Panic of 1873, which triggered inflation and bank failures across much of Europe and North America, caught up to California in the summer of 1875, up to and including ruinous speculation fever on the Comstock Lode. Panic withdrawals shut down the Farmers and Merchants Bank. The Temple and Workman Bank, with its home in the magnificent Temple Block at Temple and Main Streets, closed its doors. Los Angeles pioneer and banker William Workman shot himself in his office; F.P.F. Temple, ruined, had a stroke and died. Land sales dramatically slowed.

And yet recovery was on the way. The 1870s were a great decade for Los Angeles boosterism. Charles Nordhoff published *California: For Health, Pleasure, and Residence* in 1873, which promoted Southern California's curative climate, and over the course of the decade the infirm, inspired, arrived in droves. The citrus industry sold the orange as a metaphor for the California dream, for the orange was, as Carey McWilliams years later said, "the gold nugget of Southern California." Most importantly, in September 1876, the Southern Pacific Railroad linked Los Angeles to San Francisco, opening a transcontinental rail connection. The development of the first streetcars in 1874 boosted urban expansion. New arrivals to Los Angeles began to spread out from around the plaza.

Architecturally, Los Angeles was dominated by the vernacular of its Spanish past. Los Angeles had numerous American settlers during the Mexican era, but they adopted the local building style. The houses and commercial structures were for the most part single-story adobe, flat-roofed, and covered in brea—the tar that bubbles up from pits west of town, mixed with rocks and horsehair—with a sheltering *corredor* running along the front. Pitched red tile roofs were rare, though pitched roofs covered in shake were seen with greater frequency after the first sawmill was opened in San Bernardino in 1851.

After California was annexed to the United States, homebuilders, aided by illustrated weeklies

Upper Hill Street, near First Street. Circa 1875. An area of modest homes before the construction of the Bradbury Mansion and Bixby House.

and lithographs sold in dry goods stores, sought to build "picturesque" cottages of their own, reflecting East Coast styles. The gabled roofs of Victorian Folk style, affixed with spindlework, and the bracketed eaves of the Italianate style, began to dot the landscape in the 1850s; the prodigious French community constructed dwellings in the popular mansard-roofed Empire style. The Gothic Revival was the style of choice for those still under the sway of architectural and landscape theorist Andrew Jackson Downing, who published enormously influential treatises throughout the early 1850s on moral betterment through thoughtfully designed cottages. The transcontinental railroad brought carpenters, turners, and glaziers into town as the lumber schooners delivered endless board-feet of redwood and old-growth Douglas fir to Banning's docks in Wilmington. With plans and materials in hand, many homebuilders looked to the newly subdivided Bunker Hill to put down roots.

The homes built along Hill Street and atop Bunker Hill in the 1870s and into the mid-1880s were primarily designed in the Folk Victorian and Italianate styles. Folk Victorian was some of the earliest and simplest construction on the Hill. Most often these houses displayed a gable front and side wing, with spindlework detailing on the porch. The Italianate style derived from the Picturesque movement, which sought through asymmetry, variety, and texture to inspire the sublime. Italianate style was modeled on the rural Italian farmhouse and was marked by tall windows with elaborate crowns, wide bracketed eaves, low hipped roofs, and single story porches. Along with Gothic Revival, Italianate style was promoted by Andrew Jackson Downing as the right and true American architectural expression, as opposed to the prevailing formality and exactitude of the Greco-Roman model.

Looking across Second Street up Olive Street. In the foreground, 426 and 428 West Second St.; up Olive, 226 South Olive and its neighbor, 230/232 (with the "M"-shaped roof), and across the street, 227 South Olive. Circa 1885.

Essence of Sunshine and Noir

Other sections of the city that are growing rapidly are the Beaudry highlands, and the hills threaded by Olive, Temple, Hill, and Hope streets, and Bunker Hill avenue. This latter section is the Nob Hill of Los Angeles. The homes recently built here are the most modern class, and possess many attractions, not least among which, to the lover of the picturesque, is the marvelous view to be had from these heights. On clear days, across the broad and sunny plains, beyond the olive groves, vineyards, and gardens the sea is plainly visible, its silver surface shining between the breaks in the hills. — *Los Angeles Times*, June 22, 1883

Architecture of the Boom Years

To those who remember the unpretentious buildings erected in this city fourteen years ago, when a one-story building was considered fine, and a two-story edifice was worthy of admiration, the change to the present styles of architecture must be most noticeable and interesting. In all parts of the city the new styles of architecture, that require largely increased expense, are everywhere to be seen. The styles are almost innumerable. The Queen Anne, the Arabesque, the Moorish, the Italian, the Gothic, with variations by French architects, the Oriental, the Grecian, the English cottage style, are all abroad, producing a wonderful variety, that is most attractive and interesting. Should the present prosperity of the city be unchecked, it will soon show the most delightful varieties of architecture of any American city…from present appearances Los Angeles will soon be the most beautiful city in the world. The old style of Egyptian and Doric architecture that prevailed so long in Boston and New York will never give their funeral aspects to Los Angeles, and the Corinthian and Ionic will have to accept radical variations in this 'sun-kissed land.'" *Los Angeles Herald*, September 17, 1887

The great homes we equate with Bunker Hill were largely built in a very narrow time period, primarily between 1886 and 1889. This was a great boom time for Los Angeles. The Santa Fe Railroad brought in a second transcontinental line in 1886, giving the Southern Pacific some competition. A rate war between the two railroads drove the price of an immigrant's train ticket down to absurd lows; the price of passage from Kansas City to Los Angeles in March 1887 famously dropped to $1. Midwestern migrants came in droves, clutching Nordhoff's *California for Health, Pleasure, and Residence: A Book for Travelers and Settlers* and Charles Dudley Warner's *Our Italy*—the founding documents of California boosterism—and were met at the station by subdividers and real estate agents. They came to take in the curative climate, practice gentleman farming, bask in the glow of the wondrous orange, and dive into the romance of the "days of the dons," torn from the pages of Helen Hunt Jackson's 1884 novel *Ramona*. Los Angeles's population soared from roughly 11,000 to 80,000 by 1887.

As the population expanded, building intensified on the Hill. However, most homes were built by established Angelenos rather than new transplants, as the well-to-do sought to escape the increasingly congested residential neighborhoods and move above the effluvia. Hill Street, which ran along Bunker Hill's eastern flank, had become increasingly commercial. The noise and clamor of the commercial district abutted the industrial district along the river. Wealthy residents felt it necessary to rise above the din and dismal conditions—not just on a symbolic level, but to avoid the deadly "miasmatic" air below. Though germ theory largely replaced miasma theory in the 1880s, the idea that many diseases were airborne—communicable via the urban ghetto—was a principal tenet of many medical practitioners, including pioneering nurse Florence Nightingale.

Mining and real estate magnate Lewis Leonard Bradbury moved to Los Angeles to help his asthma. His magnificent Queen Anne residence at Court and Hill Streets, designed by Samuel and Joseph Cather Newsom and built in 1886, featured carved panels of California oak and desert cactus above the balcony and entrance.

Bunker Hill, Los Angeles

Rose Mansion—a tour de force of Queen Anne irregularity—was designed by Curlett, Eisen & Cuthbertson and built in the summer of 1887. Circa 1890.

As new construction began to increase, Bunker Hill residents felt that the correct and proper expression for their houses was the architectural style known as Queen Anne. Queen Anne coincided with architectural subsets of the Victorian styles Eastlake and Stick. Eastlake-style architecture, named for the English architect Charles Locke Eastlake, was a robust style with more angular elements than curved, especially in the bays and verandas; mansard-roofed porches, often with cresting; the style is ultimately expressed in surface ornamentation, usually seen in the application of strapwork. Similarly, the Stick style primarily features abundant millwork, or "stick-work," in a decorative structural overlay, often in a half-timbered effect not unlike Tudor, along with projecting square bays, and a vertical emphasis through the use of boards, posts, lintels, and battens. The Queen Anne style is instantly recognizable, with its asymmetry, profusion of porches and towers, turrets, and balconies, combination of siding materials, and ornamental elements, like spindles, finials, sawn bargeboards, and patterned chimneys. It was picturesque, artistic, and thus in line with Charles Eastlake's moralizing about aesthetics. All three styles came to prominence with the 1876 Centennial Exposition in Philadelphia, though Stick/Eastlake are generally considered contributors to Queen Anne.

The Queen Anne style, with its towers and half-timbering, looks quaint and antiquated to our

Bunker Hill, Los Angeles

eyes; to be sure, it had purposefully passé visual elements. Its popularity was established through the influence of Great Britain's fair buildings at the 1876 Philadelphia Centennial Exhibition, designed by Richard Norman Shaw, that featured the half-timbered and heavily patterned styles of England's Elizabethan and Jacobean eras. It should be noted that while "Queen Anne" is so named, the style in fact borrows from the Elizabethan and Jacobean, or roughly those years from 1550–1620; the architecture under the *actual* monarch Queen Anne, who ruled in the early eighteenth century, was late baroque. Architect Shaw named the style because to him and his followers, Anne's pre-Georgian reign, from 1702–1714, was the last time England had been rural and peaceful, and as such connoted the opposite to the modern industrialized world.

Despite its historical revivalism—Tudor half-timbering, monumental patterned brick chimneys, the heavily picturesque application of spindlework—the Queen Anne house was quite modern for its time. Queen Anne's profusion of millwork, for all its antique charm, was a result of the Industrial Revolution. None of it came from the handcraft tradition; the materials came from shops using power tools to produce latticework, finials, and balustrades in mass quantities. Queen Anne's asymmetrical ground plans resulted from the development of the new balloon-frame system of construction, whereby the traditional method of large timbers and hewn joints was abjured in favor of two-by-fours fastened together by that most modern of contrivances, the machine-made nail. This allowed architecture to become more liberated and structurally expressive, giving it a type of willful irregularity. The irregular exterior massing extended itself to the interior, which allowed for flexible, informal interiors. Compared to the regimented interiors of Federal architecture, the rambling Queen Anne delivered a new experience of domestic living—some two hundred years of comparative similarity and relative simplicity in the floorplans of American housing from Colonial through Greek Revival were blown apart and reconfigured.

Queen Anne houses emphasized the importance of natural light and fresh air. Modern glass-production technology allowed for larger windows, providing the Queen Anne house with greater light and air than had been allowed in previous styles—the style encouraged designers to add ample sleeping porches. The houses of the day were often praised for being well ventilated, especially in an era when most hygienic problems were thought to stem from stale, "miasmatic" air.

The Hill's late-Victorian denizens were not just fashionable to live in such houses, but were cutting-edge in including contemporary conveniences for comfort and hygienic living unthinkable one generation previous. They featured furnaces for steam and hot water, previously the exclusive domain of the very rich, and were lit by gas and electricity. Perhaps most important, because Bunker Hill was a brand-new subdivision, all of the houses had flushable, ventilated ceramic toilets connected to the municipal wastewater system.

The Queen Anne house, despite its roots in exuberant historicism, was a unique and modern expression of material prosperity and technological ingenuity. As Queen Annes were a vernacular architecture—that is, often built without aid of an architect, and not being academic in nature—the style became an easy target of scorn by "serious" architectural academics. The style quickly fell out of fashion as Classical Revival took hold in the 1890s. With the advent of the machine age, which emphasized a streamlined futurism, Queen Anne was seen as an embarrassment, and, in the postwar era, Queen Anne was at best a joke: consider the 1960s television program *The Munsters*, where a Queen Anne house was fit only for literal monsters. It was only in the late 1960s that there began a burgeoning preservation movement, but by then, it was too late for Bunker Hill.

Essence of Sunshine and Noir

Transportation on the Hill

The ability to traverse the Hill was a source of frustration for residents who needed to reach their homes from below, or for city dwellers who had business on the other side of the Hill. Some thoroughfares, like Second Street, were marked on maps as "impassable for teams" meaning that horses could not climb them. Cable cars, of the sort for which San Francisco is famous, were seen as the appropriate answer to this problem.

The Second Street Cable Railway, which ran west from Spring Street up and over Bunker Hill to Belmont Avenue—about one and a quarter miles—opened in October 1885. The stretch between Bunker Hill Avenue and Hope Street, sloped at 27.7 degrees, was the steepest gradient of any street railway in North America. The cable railway allowed its owner-investors, the Los Angeles Improvement Company (comprised of capitalists Henry Witmer, E.A. Hall, and Jesse Yarnell), to not only provide a much needed public service, but it also happened to take people from the downtown area up and over and just west of Bunker Hill to the subdivision, called Crown Hill, which the Los Angeles Improvement Company had developed and was promoting. By the time the real estate market had cooled off in 1888, the Improvement Company had sold almost all of its 1,400 lots near the terminus of the line. Mechanical failures and the torrential rains and mudslides of December 1889 that swept away portions of its track caused its permanent closure.

Local papers had suggested a cable car line on Temple Street as early as 1882; the Temple Street Cable Car Railway Company incorporated in November 1885, the month after the Second Street Railway began operation. The Temple Street Cable Railway opened July 14, 1886, and ran along Temple

The Temple Street Cable Railway station was located at the northwest corner of Temple Street and East Edgeware Road. Circa 1890.

◀◀ **Looking east on Second Street from Grand Avenue. Between Olive and Hill Streets, the turnout where the two cars of the Second Street Cable Railway pass each other. Circa 1887.**

Essence of Sunshine and Noir

The Temple Street rail car moves between Bunker and Fort Moore Hill, heading west along Temple toward Angeleno Heights. Circa 1887.

▶▶ An early photo of Angels Flight. This image was shot between November 1903, when Colonel Eddy raised the Flight's track, and the fall of 1904, when he helped finance construction of the Hillcrest Hotel, adjacent to the Flight's pavilion.

Street between Main Street and Belmont, in a little valley between Bunker Hill and Fort Moore Hill. The Temple railway later extended up to Hoover Street and connected with the Cahuenga Valley Railroad, a steam train to Hollywood.

In 1898, Pacific Electric railroad magnate and real estate developer Henry Huntington purchased the Temple Street Cable Car Railway line, and swapped its cables for an electrical system in the fall of 1901. Huntington's interests lay in extending the reach of the Pacific Electric Railway Company's cars beyond the immediate area around Bunker and Crown Hills and Angeleno Heights, and after the Temple Street Cable company was officially absorbed by Pacific Electric, he replaced the cable cars with his streetcars in November 1902.

Angels Flight

Residents of Bunker Hill at the turn of the twentieth century shared a common problem: a steep walk up and down a narrow switchback of stairs between Hill and Olive Streets. The Second Street Cable Railway had recently fallen into ruin. Hill Street was becoming increasingly commercial, and Bunker Hill itself had yet to add the number of small markets that would open around 1905–1910, so residents faced a daunting endeavor as they tended to business in the city below.

Colonel James Ward Eddy stepped up to the task. The Colonel—his military rank gained during time spent as Lincoln's bodyguard during the Civil War—was a restless sixty-nine-year-old widower, a recent transplant to Los Angeles, and a retired railroad man. In May 1901, Eddy approached the city council with an idea: a funicular that would run up Third Street, paid for out of his own pocket.

The Los Angeles Electric Incline Railway—a funicular whose biblically named cars "Olivet" and "Sinai" would forever be known as "Angels Flight"—made its inaugural trip on December 31, 1901. Mayor Meredith Snyder was the Flight's first passenger to ascend that 325-foot, 33% grade, a one-minute trip up, and another minute down. From there, Angels Flight was an enormous hit. It shuttled Hill residents, to be sure; but its role as a piece of twentieth-century technological utopianism was cemented immediately. The Flight consisted of counterbalanced cars running up and down the incline railway, each fixed to a cable attached to the fifty-horsepower motorized pulley in the station house at the top. The single track bows out mid-span allowing Olivet and Sinai to pass each other on their trips up and down the Hill.

There was also a manicured park above Clay Street called Angels Rest, which featured a 100-foot steel observation tower called Angels View, topped with a camera obscura providing a view of the city inside a darkroom. While Angels Flight served a simple purpose—getting people up to the Hill—it also engendered no small measure of civic pride. Countless postcards of the Angels Flight works were printed, purchased, and mailed home. Tourists took Angels Flight to the observation deck above. In 1912, Colonel Eddy, now eighty, sold the enterprise to the Funding Company of California for $80,000 (the equivalent of roughly $2.15 million in 2020) in cash, stocks, and bonds, leaving a comfortable fortune to his family; he passed away in 1916.

Bunker Hill, Los Angeles

The pavilion, power house, and office on Olive Street was completed in September 1910. The six-bay pavilion was reduced to two in October 1914. Circa 1911.

▲▲ Located at Third and Hill, Angels Flight has been "canyonized" over time. Angels Rest, also known as Eddy Park, has become overgrown. The observation tower was demolished in 1938. 1949.

Angels Flight had some changes over the years—the "jog" at Clay Street was replaced in 1903 with an elevated track, at which point her cream-colored, open-air cars were swapped for enclosed ones (to be famously painted orange and black in the mid-1920s). In 1910, noted architects Train & Williams were hired to design the Flight's Beaux-Arts station house on Olive and the Doric-columned lower arch on Hill Street; both were built by the California Ornamental Brick Company.

Angels Flight persevered by and large without incident (derailing once in 1913, and killing a sailor walking up the tracks in 1943) until 1969. Then, the City of Los Angeles removed and stored Angels Flight as part of the Redevelopment Plan for the Bunker Hill Urban Renewal Project. Angels Flight returned twenty-seven years later in February 1996, though not at its original location at Third and Hill (because of the late-1970s construction of the Angelus Plaza retirement community) but one-half block south on Hill Street toward Fourth Street. The City, however, decided that Edwardian technology, which functioned perfectly over the funicular's operative sixty-eight years, required updating, and subsequently engaged Lift Engineering, a ski-lift company uniquely ill-suited for the job: they had had a dozen lawsuits involving collapsing ski lifts, broken cables, seventy-plus injuries, and multiple wrongful deaths. Nevertheless, the Flight's original technology was swapped for Lift's modern cables, drums, and gears. In 2001, Lift Engineering's equipment malfunctioned: the two cars crashed into one another, and the collision killed Leon Praport, an eighty-three-year-old man who had survived the Holocaust, but not Los Angeles's attempts at modernity. After the accident, Angels Flight spent nine years sitting fallow. Reopened briefly in 2010, Angels Flight was closed in 2011 and 2013, again due to failures with its advanced technology.

After a four-year shutdown by the Public Utilities Commission, its mechanisms were updated again, with a new braking system and software design. The first ride on the restored Angels Flight was taken by Mayor Eric Garcetti on August 31, 2017, just as the initial ride on Angels Flight was taken by Mayor Snyder on December 31, 1901. The beloved funicular has since transported tourists fascinated with Old Los Angeles and the occasional local with some need to ascend the Hill.

Bunker Hill, Los Angeles

Court Flight

There were dual funiculars in the Bunker Hill area—in the region sometimes referred to as Court Hill, or the part of Bunker Hill that runs between First and Temple Streets, there was a companion to Angels Flight. Known as Court Flight, it was located adjacent to the Broadway Hotel at 205 North Broadway. It was the brainchild of Samuel G. Vandergrift and his Observation Tower Company. Vandergrift broke ground in December 1904 and built a 180-foot, 2'6" parallel two-track funicular that rose to a 335-foot elevation at a 52% grade. The two cars saved riders 141 steps up to the dead end of Court Street, just east of Hill. Vandergrift ran the flight until his death in 1932, after which his widow Annie took control.

While Court Flight was intended as a tourist operation and to serve the homeowner and apartment dwellers above, Annie relied mostly on courthouse workers and other Civic Center habitués journeying up to the parking lots through the 1930s and into World War II. During the war, however, finding reliable operators proved difficult. The little incline railway began to run at a loss. And then suddenly, in October 1943, a carelessly tossed cigarette destroyed Court Flight. Wrote the *Los Angeles Times*:

> Sparks raced speedily in the palms and underbrush and onto the ties of the old cable car line…and many a pioneer resident paused in the Civic Center to reminisce in sorrow… lawyers, judges, veterans in public services left their offices to see flames adding their fury to help erase another bit of the past from a streamlined Los Angeles.

▼▼ **A penny postcard of the Hotel Broadway shows the side-by-side cars of Court Flight. Circa 1925.**

Court Flight, gone. July 1949.

▶▶ For the 1903 Touraine apartments, 447 South Hope St., Arthur L. Haley designed a building in florid Greek Revival: wide balconies, roof balustrades, Corinthian columns, plenty of modillions and dentils, and a large pediment.

Building Resumes: Beaux-Arts Comes to the Hill

While not as numerous, apartments and hotels sprang up on the Hill contemporaneously with single-family houses. They catered to the traveler who sought renewed vigor from the life-giving Los Angeles climate, and in language reflecting the boosterism of the day, hotel advertisements often touted "sunny rooms." An advertisement for St. Angelo Hotel in October 1888 claimed:

> Pleasure Seekers or Tourists—Looking for a good, healthy elevated place to spend a few months, ought to take a look at the St. Angelo, on Grand Avenue, near Temple. Highest, healthiest locality of any hotel in Los Angeles.

Building on Bunker Hill took a hiatus when, after a speculative land boom, banks tightened their loan policies, and land promoters became overextended. Following the real estate bust of the late 1880s, there came the Panic of 1893, caused by railroad overbuilding and failure, and the Sherman Silver Purchase Act. With the collapse of major employers and the subsequent national economic crisis, American unemployment leapt from 3% to 18%. Banks closed. When Los Angeles emerged from its economic doldrums, tastes had changed: the Brooklyn *Daily Eagle* wrote in 1899 that Queen Anne style was

> tiresome and homely, result[ing] in grotesque and sometimes hideous constructions of a higglety-pigglety class of architecture in which every style was mixed up and no style either predominated or appeared to good effect.

During this time America witnessed the ascendency of architect Richard Morris Hunt, the first American admitted to and trained at the École des Beaux-Arts. Hunt championed Renaissance forms and the grandeur of Europe as the correct visual language for the formal, grandiose "cottages" he designed for the scions of the Gilded Age. These influenced the eclectic classicism of architects McKim, Mead, and White, who adopted Greco-Roman forms in their many grand public buildings.

A major influence on the era was the 1893 Chicago World's Fair, also known as the World's Columbian Exposition, which spurred a classical revival in America. The Chicago fair promulgated the tenets of the City Beautiful movement, which sought to clean up the chaos of America's tenements via order, dignity, and harmony based on a neoclassical model. The "White City," as the fair was known, featured acres of titanic, totemic Beaux-Arts buildings in gleaming plaster of Paris. The fair was supervised by pioneering modernist architects Burnham and Root, who fixed the popular taste for equating America with the majesty of imperial Rome. The Exposition also promoted Colonial Revival through structures that reimagined the iconic American features of Mount Vernon and Independence Hall. The Idaho Building famously prefigured the Arts and Crafts movement, and Mission Revival architecture took hold in the collective imagination via the California State Building.

At the same time, the enormously influential Edward Bok, who wielded a powerful voice as editor of *Ladies' Home Journal* (which in 1895 began reproducing house plans in its pages), waged a war against what Bok termed the "repellently ornate." Bok crusaded against the Queen Anne style, stating that it lacked taste and refinement, and asserting that its gaudiness was luridly akin to circus wagons. Other governing tastemakers of the day, like Elsie de Wolfe—America's first interior decorator—and Edith Wharton, whose 1897 book *Decoration of Houses* denounced all things Victorian, caused Americans to consider Queen Anne style hopelessly lowbrow. Its replacement would contain none of the

asymmetrical facades of the previously popular "Elizabethan Cottage Style," as the Queen Anne was often termed. They emphasized Classical design principles, Beaux-Arts styling, and relied heavily on inspiration from 18th-century France for interior decoration. Their rejection of Queen Anne was to be just as eclectic and revivalist, to be sure, deriving from neoclassical and Greek revival styles. New construction would involve no small quantity of bilateral symmetry, columns, and pediments.

The fate of Elden Patrick Bryan's grand Victorian mansion at 333 South Grand Ave. is a representative example of Bunker Hill's aesthetic shift from Queen Anne to Beaux-Arts. Bryan came from Texas as a cotton merchant, part of the 1886 boom, but shifted his focus to real estate upon arriving in Los Angeles, developing tracts in what are now the Pico-Union and MacArthur Park neighborhoods, and earning his fortune in part by selling lots to railroad tycoon Henry Huntington. In 1888, Bryan hired vaunted architect Joseph Cather Newsom to design a rambling, shingled Queen Anne manse. But Bryan was developing Westmoreland Place, a gated residential subdivision three miles west, where he had architect Charles F. Whittlesey design an eighteen-room mansion in a blend of Mission, Tudor, and Japanese—styles that further came to define Los Angeles, and the amalgam of which was for better or worse particularly Angelenic. Bryan sold the house on Grand Avenue in February 1902 to H.C. Norris, who in turn sold it to the father-and-son development team of Joseph and Robert Marsh in April 1903. The Marshes demolished the house and hired Fred R. Dorn to design the Fleur-de-Lis, a small family hotel with thirty-nine rooms, erected at the end of 1903. Where there was once a riot of angles and patterns in the great tradition of a Newsom Queen Anne, there was now a perfectly ordered, symmetrical façade with a heavy corbelled pediment and Ionic columns, topped by an imposing balustrade.

The Bryan residence on South Grand Avenue designed by Joseph Cather Newsom may hold the record for the shortest-lived of the major houses built on the Hill; it lasted a mere fifteen years.

▶▶ The Dorn-designed Fleur-de-Lis, 1903. Renamed the Capitol Hotel in 1921, it was demolished in 1964. Image circa 1904.

Bunker Hill, Los Angeles

Mission Revival on the Hill

Mission Revival was another dominant architectural style on the Hill that existed concurrently with the Beaux-Arts. The 1893 World's Columbian Exposition had not only inspired Americans to look to European classical models, it exposed an international audience to the Mission style's hallmarks. The missions of Alta California had been a product of Franciscan priests' architectural background in Spain and Colonial Mexico City, combining Renaissance and baroque ideals with the limited local building materials such as adobe and clay. From these elements, the Franciscans developed the familiar characteristics of unadorned plaster surfaces, clay roof tiles, thick arches, long exterior arcades, semi-independent bell gables, and the baroque gables with towers popularly associated with the California mission chain.

The Fair's Texas and California State Buildings, both executed in Mission Revival style, were enormously influential; A. Page Brown's California Pavilion, based loosely on Mission Santa Barbara, proved to be enormously popular, and influenced people to consider the Mission style an appropriate expression of the American West's Colonial past, much in the way Georgian features were revived in the Northeast's Colonial Revival. Thus, for much of the Hill's building boom of 1902–1906, architects worked within this historical narrative, and looked to nostalgia for an indigenous past for their visual language, using an assemblage of recurrent hallmarks (stucco walls, scalloped parapets, red tile, quatrefoil windows, and bell towers) to impart a Californian cultural identity.

Period boosterism played up the picturesque nature of Southern California, with an emphasis on

Arthur L. Haley prepared plans for Hotel Munn in September 1902. It featured a foliate scroll frieze below two red-tiled towers and a quatrefoil inside a scalloped parapet. Circa 1903.

Essence of Sunshine and Noir

regional history, often with a nod to the missions themselves. Helen Hunt Jackson's widely read works praised the missions; in her 1883 *Glimpses of California and the Missions*, she writes of Mission Carmel:

> … its ruins have to-day a charm far exceeding all the others. The fine yellow tint of the stone, the grand and unique contour of the arches, the beautiful star-shaped window in the front, the simple yet effective lines of carving on pilaster and pillar and doorway, the symmetrical Moorish tower and dome, the worn steps leading up to the belfry,—all make a picture whose beauty, apart from hallowing associations, is enough to hold one spell-bound.

Jackson romanticizes the state of ruination into which the missions had fallen; their neglect leant an elegiac, wistful angle to the shared awareness that they had deteriorated, perhaps beyond repair. Charles Fletcher Lummis, indefatigable booster of the Southwest, called the missions "the best capital Southern California has" and emphasized the "comfort, security, and picturesqueness" of the Mission style in an 1895 article titled "The Lesson of the Adobe." This was published in his promotional journal *Land of Sunshine*. Renamed *Out West* in 1902, the magazine represented California's passion for all things Mission, and promoted conservation and preservation of early California history.

Mission Revival was the first style to start in the West and spread east; between 1900 and 1925, countless homes, hotels, schools, and train stations embraced the style for its simplicity and dignity. The Santa Fe Railway, in particular, designed Mission Revival stations along its routes. Homebuyers across the country enjoyed the romantic associations, and homebuilders were pleased with how the style was easy to pair with the era's newfound love of concrete.

Mission style was significant on the Hill between 1902 and 1905. Prior to this time, in the late 1890s, Los Angeles had seen the construction of some major examples of Mission Revival buildings. These were primarily residential, like John Kremple's house for General Harrison Gray Otis (1898) and Frederick L. Roehrig's oft-published W.C. Stuart house of 1895, plus commercial projects like the Hollenbeck Home for the Aged (Morgan and Walls, 1896), the Hotel Green Annex (Frederick L. Roehrig, 1898), and Long Beach High School (George Costerisan, 1898). Mission Revival in Los Angeles reached its zenith about 1906 when it fell out of favor, eclipsed by the Craftsman style, Beaux-Arts, and other revivalist styles. Few major works in the Mission style are built around the Los Angeles area after 1910, save for Julia Morgan's Examiner Building of 1912. For some, the Pueblo Revival, which approximated the regional vernacular of the Southwest with its earth-tone "adobe" (concrete) walls and projecting roof beams, was seen as closer to a "true" American architecture. For most, the Spanish Colonial was a welcome variant. While the Mission style fell out of favor, its unadorned surfaces, indoor/outdoor living, and truthful expression of materials helped to usher in Modernism, even influencing the renowned Irving Gill, whose career as a pioneering modernist was rooted in the Mission Revival.

Life on the Hill

Early life on Bunker Hill was pastoral compared to the city below. There was bountiful wildlife upon the Hill; besides the domesticated—most houses kept stables, and horses grazed in the pastures west and below Bunker Hill Avenue—frogs were heard at night, croaking in the pond at Second and Beaudry Streets and the gulch at First Street and Grand Avenue. Badgers were once plentiful as well—in August 1887, prominent contractor John G. Hickethier fired five pistol shots at one in his backyard at 27 North Bunker Hill Ave., to the consternation of local law enforcement. People and

Bunker Hill, Los Angeles

animals escaped onto the Hill in part because the lowlands near the river were so prone to flooding.

The early days of Bunker Hill, after its initial blooming, were regularly marked by gatherings and fêtes recounted in the social columns. A *Los Angeles Times* description of a typical Hill event ran as such—a wedding on January 8, 1895:

> The wedding of Miss Ella Catherine Mills and Mr. Albert Butler Clapp, a well-known real estate man of this city, took place at the residence of the bride's parents, Mr. and Mrs. Howard Mills, 327 South Olive St. … the rooms were handsomely decorated with smilax, palms, and a profusion of flowers. Each room had a different scheme of color, that in which the ceremony took place being in safrano roses and marguerites. The bay window of the drawing room was converted into a bower of green. The bride and groom stood in this under a marriage bell composed of marguerites. In the dining room, where an elaborate supper was served, pink and green were used effectively, strands of smilax and pink ribbon extended from the chandelier to the four corners of the table; at either end of the table were candelabra holding pink candles and shades. On the mantel were handsome bowls of pink roses.

As Bunker Hill began to age, so too did its original population; the well-to-do left the Hill for new properties away from the noise of the city, where there were more respectable addresses, fewer apartment buildings, and more social cachet.

Those who stayed on the Hill grew older with the buildings. The immigrants of the 1880s—the "middle-aged, middle-class, middle-west" settlers who changed the cultural demographics of Los Angeles—became pensioners. A vigorous forty-year-old in 1887 was sixty in 1907; the average American lifespan in 1900 was forty-nine.

Residents of the Melrose Hotel, an early boarding house at 130 South Grand Ave., lounge on the porch. Circa 1895.

Essence of Sunshine and Noir

The Mills House, built in 1887 at 327 South Olive St., was demolished in August 1948 to provide a parking lot for the Ems Apartments next door. 1912.

Times and demographics continued to change. During the severe economic downturn of the 1890s, people poured into Los Angeles, doubling the population from 50,000 to 100,000, lured by the poetry of Grace Ellery Channing, the lure of Arroyo Culture as promulgated by *Land of Sunshine* magazine, and the romantic, intellectual boosterism of Charles Fletcher Lummis. After Edward Doheny struck oil in 1892, even more people flooded west hoping they too could make a fortune with their own inky strikes.

These new transplants encountered a Hill that was rapidly becoming less moneyed, less exclusive. Many residents who had built new houses during the boom had moved on. Los Angeles was being shaped by the advent of the automobile. This new mode of transport allowed residents the freedom of movement needed to expand all over the Los Angeles basin. Living near the commercial center was once seen as convenient, or a necessity, but was certainly now seen as hopelessly old-fashioned. The rich could abandon their "repellently ornate" homes for sleek Spanish and up-to-date Craftsman houses or live in the flatlands of newly subdivided Windsor Square, because even the concept of living on a hill above the effluvia seemed terribly … well, Victorian.

As the hoi polloi moved in, the social fabric changed. Where did all the fine families go? A study of the social registers tells the story. There were two competing registers that were virtually identical: *The Southwestern Blue Book, A Society Directory*, and the *Los Angeles Blue Book, Social Register of Southern California*, these being the rosters of patrician families of best breeding, so that members of high society might know who else belonged to their tribe. In the 1894–1895 edition of the *Los Angeles Blue Book*, thirty-nine of its socialites live on Bunker Hill/Fort Moore Hill. By 1916, the *Southwestern Blue Book* only lists six. Mrs. B.F. Coulter had moved to Berkeley Square; the Bannings relocated to West Adams; William Lacy built his Hunt & Eager-designed Tudor house at the corner of Wilshire and Vermont in 1906. Many former residents now lived in St. James Park, Chester Place, or the Avenues in Highland Park; the 1916 edition has large sections devoted to the newly fashionable areas of Beverly Hills, Glendale, Hollywood, Altadena, etc. The only two entries in both books, spanning two decades, are Earl Millar, at Third and Olive Streets, and Fanny Mills on Fort Moore Hill.

By the 1920s, the population of the Hill lived on increasingly meager means. They were sequestered from the rest of town by the physical separation the Hill afforded, but while living above the fray was once a plus, as residents aged, distance became a challenge. Those with the resources to depart did so, and working-class people moved in. There was an increasing influx of Hispanic people, primarily north of First Street, and a neighborhood of Native Americans along Clay Street.

Bunker Hill slowly became a place out of time. The newspapers began to note this in the 1920s. In a September 1925 article titled "Hill Keeps Denizens From Bustle of City" by *Los Angeles Times* writer P.H. Gartner, the journalist writes that he had never been up on the Hill, that it "must be of some use to somebody," and made a visit. He called it "an entirely different world." Describing the intricate ornament and spacious yards, he noted especially that families sat together to

> spend the evening in the quiet manner of their grandparents… With the peace of years ago in the air, one can sit alone in the little green park at the head of the Hill Street tunnel and

Bunker Hill, Los Angeles

watch the foolish motorists below spend their precious minutes wrestling a crossing from one another, intent on their petty affairs.

Conversely, another *Los Angeles Times* writer, Eva G. Taylor, bemoaned the loss of Los Angeles's "atmosphere," in 1926, noting that before World War I, Bunker Hill had yet to be invaded by auto-repair shops, and noble old flowering trees had not been lost to apartment houses, and "even as late as the beginning of this century much of the old charm lingered. Bunker Hill with its stately homes was a spot where the newly arrived Easterner found his dreams of beautiful Los Angeles realized. The exodus to the south and west had yet hardly begun."

In April 1936, *Los Angeles Times* writer L.D. Murtagh, a Hill resident, wrote a piece called "No Pity Wanted—On Bunker Hill" in which he defended his neighborhood. He described the madness of the adjacent, teeming city:

> yet up here there reigns a calm that is almost anesthetic…the quiet of the hill is an anodyne for shattered nerves…for this is a place of far horizons where one may know a mystic mood or think a lofty thought, undisturbed by the cacophonies of a mechanical civilization. It is even possible to sit on the bench at the top of Third Street and slip imperceptibly into a pleasant sleep.

A quiet day on Bunker Hill, looking north on Grand Avenue. The apartment houses have begun to take hold. At far left, the twin gables of the Brunson Mansion tower over its lawn. Its neighbor, the hotel Fleur-de-Lis, is flush with the sidewalk. Circa 1913.

Essence of Sunshine and Noir

▲ John Fante's home, the Alta Vista, at 255 South Bunker Hill Ave. It was developed by father-daughter developer team James and Maud Shields, with architectural designs by James. 1957.

▲▲ Pensioners on the porch of the Alta Vista. 1955.

Murtagh likened the Hill to "an ivory tower" which "in spite of progress, will retain its Olympian calm. A sanctuary of quiet in the very center of a great city. What other city in the world can boast of such a hill?" Murtagh goes on to make a lengthy and eloquent case for the Hill's winds being more persistent and soothing, its trees more beautiful, its automobiles better behaved, and its community more tightly knit than anywhere else—"one has the illusion of strolling down a village street. The little stores have a friendly atmosphere … the Hill is friendly to lovers and here they may be as much alone as if they strolled down a country lane."

Novelist John Fante lived on the Hill in 1933–1934 and captured, in his romantic fiction, its aging charm. Fante's *Ask the Dust*, his quintessential 1939 *roman à clef* about Los Angeles, introduced Bunker Hill to the world at large, and would prove influential on writers and filmmakers who followed. Novelist and poet Charles Bukowski, who came to define a raw and unvarnished Los Angeles, considered Fante his "God," and as he began to write, would stare up at Bunker Hill, obsessing over his deity. Robert Towne read *Ask the Dust* in an attempt to understand the authentic voice of Los Angeles as he wrote *Chinatown*; Towne called *Ask the Dust* "the greatest novel ever written about Los Angeles" and made it into a motion picture in 2006. In *Ask the Dust*, Fante renamed his home at Third Street and Grand Avenue, the Alta Vista, the "Alta Loma." It was here Fante lived when he described his room in *Ask the Dust* as inside an apartment house "built on a hillside in reverse, there on the crest of Bunker Hill." Fante's alter ego Arturo Bandini would climb out of his window midway down the Hill toward Hope Street, and walk up the slope to Bunker Hill Avenue, on "a night for my nose, a feast for my nose, smelling the stars, across the top of Bunker Hill. The city spread out like a Christmas tree, red and green and blue." Fante-as-Bandini would walk "down the street toward Angels Flight, wondering what I would do that day" and, after some misadventures, make his way home:

> Up the dusty stairs of Bunker Hill, past the soot-covered frame buildings along that dark street…Dust and old buildings and old people sitting at windows, old people tottering out of doors, old people moving painfully along the dark street. The old folk from Indiana and Iowa and Illinois, from Boston and Kansas City and Des Moines, they sold their homes and their stores, and they came here by train and by automobile to the land of sunshine, to die in the sun, with just enough money to live until the sun killed them…

Bunker Hill, Los Angeles

Fante wrote a piece for the *Times* in June 1940 titled "Goodbye, Bunker Hill," in which he further described his time there, living on fruit from the grocery store at Third and Flower, tapping out stories on his typewriter in the Alta Vista.

> It held me, that mysterious little room with its startling view, that lonely Bunker Hill with its ancient buildings, its quiet streets and lonely trees with here and there a bright spot from which came the scent of singing hamburgers … the high frightened squeal of the cable car lurching up Angels Flight.
>
> I was higher than the City Hall, higher than the Biltmore, higher than the Richfield Tower. It was paradise.

Fante described the tenants of the Alta Vista, the alcoholics, the gaunt packrats, the working girl ejected for plying her trade, the Theosophist draped in black, and the other budding novelists, who would return home in the evening, breathing hard after climbing up the hill, and throw themselves into the porch rockers. "The quiet hill relaxed them, the swishing, grease-stained palms told them they had returned to their earth again, back from the crazy whirl below. Their limbs sang with gratitude for Bunker Hill…" Fante wrote despairingly that—and this was years before the word was made flesh, with the establishment of the redevelopment agency—the papers insisted the Hill was to be torn down in the name of progress.

In the postwar era, the *Los Angeles Times*, always quick to condemn the Hill for its decrepitude and promote redevelopment, was not, even then, averse to its charms. In his 1952 piece "Romance Dwells Atop Bunker Hill, City's Treasure Chest of Yesterday," Harry Nelson wrote:

> Life is rich in the dozen square blocks atop Bunker Hill. It's rich in the things that artists and poets and writers call wealth. Things like picturesque old buildings, a romantic past and human interest drama … the people of the Hill begin to emerge. The children to play, the late churchgoers to church, the winos to the liquor stores, the old cronies to sit on the benches by the Alta Vista Hotel on Bunker Hill Ave. Along 1st St. old Mexicans in cone-shape, broad-brimmed sombreros and teen-agers in zoot suits lounge around the corners to joke and shout to one another from across the street.

In 1956, USC film student Kent Mackenzie—best known for his 1961 feature *The Exiles*, shot largely on Bunker Hill—produced an eighteen-minute documentary titled *Bunker Hill 1956*. It is arguably the most accurate filmed depiction of life on the Hill, shooting the lives of a druggist, doctor, and carpenter without an ideological agenda, depicting its subjects in the true and common lives they led. *Bunker Hill 1956* follows the course of a typical day on the Hill and as night descends, it is refreshing to see merrymaking commence at the Café Montana in the New Grand Hotel at 255 South Grand Ave.; normally, were cameramen to be on Bunker Hill in the mid-1950s, they were capturing a very different type of narrative; e.g., 1955's *Kiss Me Deadly* or 1956's *The Killing*.

Bunker Hill traditionally has been seen in black and white, often via the images of photographers like Arnold Hylen or William Reagh, whose photographs spurred interest in the Hill when placed online in the 1990s. Arnold Hylen is probably the best known of the Hill chroniclers. Hylen trained at Chouinard and the Pasadena Art Institute and worked for the Fluor Corporation, photographing the company's oil refineries and chemical plants. On weekends, however, from the mid-1940s

A man passes by the apartments at 512 West Second St., in an image by Hylen from *Bunker Hill: A Los Angeles Landmark*. Circa 1960.

Essence of Sunshine and Noir

Photographer William Reagh was standing atop the Broadway Tunnel, facing west toward the intersection of Hill Street, when he captured this gentleman standing on fire escape of the La Salle Apartments at 314 California St. 1940.

through the late 1960s—which Hylen termed "the swan song of early Los Angeles,"—he departed his East Los Angeles home and roamed the disappearing downtown, his Rolleiflex or Leica in hand, shooting whatever caught his eye. Dawson's Book Shop printed two books culled from these images, *Bunker Hill: A Los Angeles Landmark* (500 copies, 1976) and *Los Angeles Before the Freeways 1850–1950* (600 copies, 1981). Hylen's *Bunker Hill* is the best primary source about the Hill, providing valuable insight into life there.

William Reagh arrived in Los Angeles from Kansas in the 1930s and worked as a commercial photographer, and for decades he wandered the city on weekends, documenting its changing face. Reagh quit his job in the 1960s to devote himself full time to photography, just as the Bunker Hill redevelopment swung into full force. He photographed thousands of pictures on his wanderings, until his death in 1992, and his collection of work is especially strong in images of Bunker Hill; the length of time over which he shot allowed him to capture places as they changed over the years.

The work of Leonard Nadel, which has been made available online through the Los Angeles Public Library and the Getty Research Institute, has also contributed much to the historical record of Bunker

Hill. Nadel, with his graduate degree in education from Columbia University, relocated to Los Angeles in 1949 to become documentary photographer for the City Housing Authority and Community Redevelopment Agency. His job was to promulgate the agency's subsidized housing agenda by contrasting the decrepitude of slums with the healthy, ordered lifestyle to be had via redevelopment. His images of Bunker Hill—ramshackle backyards, the shoeless children, and hanging laundry—went a long way in the effort to justify housing clearance. However, despite the political motives behind his assignment, about half of Nadel's photographs in the CRA archives depict apartments rated as "acceptable," which contradicts the premise that the majority of Bunker Hill's housing would be rated "slum."

Despite the long shadows in the black-and-white images of Hylen and Reagh, Nadel's photographs are imbued with humanity, and show a healthy, functioning community. Similarly, the many photographs by amateur photographer Theodore Seymour Hall are full of a rich pathos, depicting children, folks shopping for groceries, and building demolitions.

Hall had an interesting history: he was the son of a prosperous Hawaiian ship chandler, Harvard-educated, worked in the chemical and mortgage industries, and through the 1930s lived in Long Island, New York, as an executive with industrial bankers National Cash Credit Association. For whatever reason, come 1940, the sixty-year-old Hall was divorced and living alone in the Sherwood Apartments at 431 South Grand Ave. It was at this time he developed an interest in photography, and became an Associate in the Photographic Society of America. In 1952, he moved to the Cumberland Hotel at 243 South Olive St., until it was emptied and demolished, so he spent his final three years at the Engstrum Apartments, 623 West Fifth St., before he died in March 1963.

A photograph by Theodore Seymour Hall depicts children with the rubble of a demolished house. Circa 1957.

Essence of Sunshine and Noir

An elderly gentleman walks north on Clay Street. November 1955.

Two women chat outside 201 South Bunker Hill Ave., in a photograph by Leonard Nadel. One has just done her shopping down at Grand Central Market. September 1955.

A sunny morning on the 300 block of South Bunker Hill Avenue. December 1961.

What was an average day on Bunker Hill like? Hylen put it cogently:

> Older citizens sat on verandas gossiping and sunning themselves on ancient pieces of furniture, or tottered leisurely to the little stores, like those on the southeast corner of Third and Grand, where there was always a fine flurry of activity on Sundays. Then too there was the usual parade of elderly church-goers, tidily dressed in a variety of rather outdated fashions, occasionally raising an eyebrow in consternation at some vagrant soul in a deserted doorway sleeping off the effects of Saturday night's revels. Others just amble casually about the streets for a sunny constitutional. Everything moved at a very relaxed tempo, much as one would suppose it was during the more leisurely past.

Hylen also wrote of the elderly as they traversed the hill:

> … the little grade from Olive down to Hill was not very steep but many of the elderly were often to be seen, some with the aid of a cane, faltering up and down the sidewalk with their meager share of purchases. It was at times a pathetic sight to see some of the aged ones, neglected in appearance and trembling with infirmity, struggling to contend with the rush of life around them. They were a helpless minority, and in the midst of present-day social and economic surroundings, their plight seemed even more conspicuous.

In contrast to the black-and-white images usually equated with the area, recently discovered color photographs challenge the conventional understanding of the Hill. Recently unearthed Bunker Hill images by the likes of Virgil Mirano, Palmer Conner, and George Mann reveal a neighborhood replete with well-tended structures, comfortable people, and flower-filled gardens. Virgil Mirano was a cinematographer who shot some three hundred slides of disappearing Victorian Los Angeles from 1957 to 1970; his collection was accessioned by the Bancroft Library in 2018. Edmund Palmer Conner, the San Gabriel title insurance/escrow businessman and real estate investor, as well as a lecturer and essayist about California rancho history, shot more than seven hundred color slides of downtown Los Angeles as it underwent transformation between 1953 and 1970; these were donated to the Huntington Library in 2010.

Unlike Mirano and Conner, who shot for their own satisfaction and delectation, George Mann shot the Hill professionally for personal gain. Mann was an ex-vaudevillian who in the 1950s became an entrepreneur, developing a 3-D viewer to be installed in coffee shops and doctors' waiting rooms. He captured various locales for his device (Catalina Island, Knott's Berry Farm, Watts Towers, etc.) but

Bunker Hill, Los Angeles

 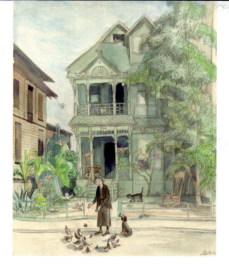 

his two dozen Bunker Hill shots reveal the area—the verdant, walkable neighborhood whose buildings are endlessly complex and whose cats are pleasantly brushed.

In 1964, Leo Politi, the Italian-American children's author, painter, and illustrator, produced a book of watercolors of the Hill called *Bunker Hill, Los Angeles: Reminiscences of Bygone Days*, wherein one of the paintings depicted a woman named Rose, who lived in "a charming old place in a rusty green color" and cared for the neighborhood animals. In 2010, Rose's story was given further depth when Mann's photograph surfaced, showing her brushing a kitty at 246 South Bunker Hill Ave., where calla lilies grow along her worn wooden stairs.

Politi wasn't the only artist to capture the Hill on canvas. In his 1952 *Times* article, Harry Nelson wrote that Bunker Hill is "a treasure chest of something else that appears to a romantic soul—memories. What about the art class, squatting on orange crates and folding stools, sketching the quaint old mansion at Fourth and Hope?" Indeed, its faded charm proved irresistible to professional and amateur alike. Leo Politi is best remembered today, and was joined on the Hill's doomed streets in its end days by the likes of Kay Martin, Ben Abril, and local residents such as Marcel Cavalla.

And near Bunker Hill's end, about the time the city council approved the CRA's tentative plan for its redevelopment, the neighborhood began to be rediscovered by the cultivated set, and the urbane element repopulated it, if only for a short time. Joan Winchell, society columnist for the *Los Angeles Times*, who moved from Brentwood to Bunker Hill, wrote about her new surroundings in July 1956:

> Bunker Hill has been called a Greenwich Village, a French Quarter, a Left Bank, a Georgetown, a Telegraph Hill and Knob Hill. But it's "Snob Hill" to the newcomers occupying the old Victorian homes recently streamlined by Fritz Burns. Florence Chase, a very chic lady, has tastefully combined traditional furnishings with contemporary. Bachelor Allan Petrie entertains Philharmonic first-nighters in his black-and-white modern apartment. Winter (nephew of Edward Everett) Horton calls his "Early Charles Adams [sic]." Can look down on Flower St. and see Pat Burns' tangerine front door … We're like a family, we "Bunker Hillbillies."

The Fritz Burns of whom she wrote was Fritz Bernard Burns, prolific residential developer and a proponent of rehabilitating Bunker Hill. Burns, with his son Patrick, had rehabbed a number of Bunker Hill houses, beginning in 1954 with the purchase of three homes built circa 1885 at 240–242 North Hope St.; the Burnses made news in stating the houses were in need of no structural repair, just some modernization. Burns was also the field service representative of ACTION: the American

Painters face south on Bunker Hill Avenue, near the corner of Third Street. Circa 1962.

Leo Politi, in his book of watercolors, described Rose and her inseparable dog, and how she took care of the Hill's wild birds—which went with her when she was forced off the Hill. Circa 1958.

Rose brushes a cat at 246 South Bunker Hill in a photograph by George Mann; there is also a photograph of Rose by Theodore Hall at the Huntington Library. Circa 1960.

Essence of Sunshine and Noir

43

Built in 1895, 129 South Flower St. is shown here painted black and white with a tangerine door. Fall 1962. At right, its living room, after modernization by Fritz Burns. 1955.

Council to Improve Our Neighborhoods. It was ACTION's contention that America's problem with slum clearance could be removed by conserving and rehabilitating existing houses and neighborhoods. Burns asserted that if owners were to bring their properties up to code, it would be unnecessary to raze Bunker Hill. To accomplish this, he purchased another home, a standard-issue Victorian house at 129 South Flower St., all board and brackets and bay windows, and painted it black with a "tangerine front door." The fourteen-foot ceilings were lowered, and partitions removed to open up rooms, and after a remodel its interior was a coolly composed scene of clean lines, white walls, primitive art, and Danish Modern furniture. Cordell Hicks—sole woman on the hundred-man City Desk at the *Times*—had with Patrick Burns pioneered the return-to-Bunker Hill movement, living in the North Hope Street apartment before the Flower Street refurbishments. Horton, Petrie, and Winchell had moved into and restored 203 and 209 South Bunker Hill Ave.; by 1960, Winchell and Hicks both lived at 129 South Flower St. Hicks told *Prompter* magazine about her upstairs apartment in October 1960: "I have a better view from my bathroom window than I would from the living room of a Bel-Air mansion!" In the same issue Winchell described her neighbors as friendly, quiet, and loyal. Bunker Hill's gentrification had begun, but the seeds of its destruction had been sown.

Bunker Hill, Los Angeles

Hill Street

One cannot study Bunker Hill without investigating Hill Street, Bunker Hill's great anchor at its eastern flank, facing the business district. Hill Street, like Bunker Hill, is a lost world. When Bunker Hill is discussed, focus is typically given to the Hill's interior, especially to the eponymous avenue lined with mansions running along its spine, and not to Calle Loma—Hill Street—so named because it ran along the base of the hill that loomed over the blooming town. On the 1849 Ord Survey map, Calle Loma runs north from Fifth Street until the Hill stops it between Second and First Streets. Eventually it was cut through, and along the eastern edge of Bunker Hill many houses were built, but as the city moved west from the Plaza, Hill Street became increasingly commercial.

Hill Street between Fifth and First Streets was once a mighty commercial thoroughfare lined with important buildings—though few remain today, as the majority were leveled along with the Hill to its west. At one time Fifth and Hill was the busiest intersection in Los Angeles (although some argued that title belonged to Seventh and Broadway, and by the mid-1930s the honor had moved west, to Wilshire and Western). Wrote the *Los Angeles Times* in April 1929:

> Nerves are on edge at Fifth and Hill at 5 o'clock in the afternoon, and at other hours. There is a vast congestion there at many times. But when the shops and stores are disgorging their thousands of workers and visitors, who suddenly discover a clamorous necessity to get home or somewhere else Fifth and Hill becomes one of the most nervous corners in Los Angeles.

Thousands streamed in and out of the Subway Terminal, or into and out of the many mighty office buildings that lined the sidewalks. As business moved away from downtown, and with the cessation of the subway in 1955, the area slid into disrepair. A 1956 police report on Bunker Hill described Hill Street as a "secondary skid row" with "bars along Hill Street notorious as hangouts for undesirables." The CRA demolished most of the hotels and office buildings soon after as part of the Bunker Hill redevelopment plan.

Essence of Sunshine and Noir

The view north on Hill Street from Fifth Street. Circa 1935.

Fort Moore Hill

The northern part of what is commonly called Bunker Hill, roughly bounded by Temple, Broadway, Figueroa, and Sunset, has its own name: Fort Moore Hill. It shares the same history as Bunker Hill—rising over Los Angeles, covered by homes after the boom, and then apartments, until it grew a bit downmarket, and then was carved up and remade after World War II. And yet the story of Fort Moore contains much more: military might, cemeteries, schools, and a race of lizard men.

During the Siege of Los Angeles in September 1846—before any of the elevated area to the west of the Plaza had a name, Captain Archibald Gillespie directed his soldiers to establish a fortification on the hill looming over the church and pueblo. Eventually a hundred-man garrison, composed of a 400-foot breastwork with bastions for cannon, was built by men of the U.S. Army Mormon Battalion. They named the fort after Captain Benjamin D. Moore, recently killed in the ill-fated charge at San Pasqual. Fort Moore was dedicated July 4, 1847, the first Independence Day celebration held in Los Angeles.

Fort Moore was decommissioned in 1853, and Fort Moore Hill became Los Angeles's first Protestant cemetery. The City took over the cemetery in 1869, failed to maintain it or keep records, and it was ordered closed in 1886. Though consecrated ground, the City began to sell off the cemetery piecemeal as residential developments, and as building lots to the Board of Education.

The first major structure was Jacob Phillippi's beer hall, the Buena Vista, built in the spring of 1883, though Mary Hollister Banning, recent widow of Phineas "Father of the Port of Los Angeles" Banning, bought and converted it to her private retreat in 1887. Soon the Queen Anne homes of Los Angeles's leading families covered an unbroken stretch from the southern tip of Bunker Hill to the northern end of Fort Moore Hill.

Looking west across Buena Vista Street to the Buena Vista tavern on North Fort Street (later Broadway). "Perfect order and the exclusion of improper characters guaranteed" ran the announcement of its opening, although the establishment took on a reputation as a roadhouse with a rough edge. Circa 1885.

▶▶ **The view from Bunker Hill: atop the Hill Street Tunnel. Hill Street Tunnel # 2, also known as North Hill Street Tunnel, can be glimpsed left-center. The large structure is the Richardsonian Romanesque high school. November 1919.**

Bunker Hill, Los Angeles

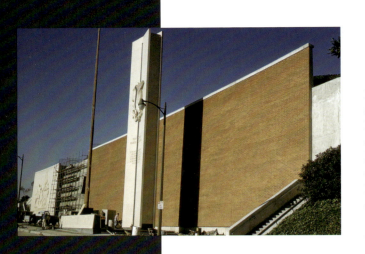

With the Fort Moore Pioneer Memorial under construction, workers on the scaffolding install some 30,000 mosaic tiles at the memorial's waterfall. February 1958.

In July 1886, Los Angeles High School was moved from nearby Poundcake Hill onto Fort Moore; it became an elementary school when a large red brick high school was built in 1890. The children of Bunker Hill and Fort Moore romped in the decaying cemetery which served as school playground. Like all of the Hill south of Temple Street, Fort Moore saw the building of apartment buildings after the turn of the century. Emma Summers, "Oil Queen of Los Angeles," built an unusual Beaux-Arts-Moorish structure called The Queen Apartments near the old school in 1906.

In the early 1930s, Fort Moore residents were treated to the spectacle of George Warren Shufelt, a geophysical engineer who lived in the Hillcrest on Bunker Hill, tunneling into the Hill in search of underground catacombs dug by the lost empire of the Lizard People, who five thousand years ago left enormous gold tablets inscribed with the origins of the human race. By the spring of 1934, he had found only mud.

Others soon dug into Fort Moore; its eastern flank was lost to the straightening of Spring Street, the proposed Civic Center expansion, and Union Station's need for dirt to fill grade in the 1930s. In the 1940s, the remainder of its buildings were taken by eminent domain and demolished in anticipation of the Hollywood Freeway, which cut through the center of Fort Moore Hill. Many bodies of Los Angeles pioneers were unearthed in the excavations.

The Fort Moore Pioneer Memorial, designed by Kazumi Adachi and Dike Nagano, was dedicated July 3, 1958. It included a waterfall, a seventy-five-foot pylon by Albert Stewart, plus a forty-five by seventy-eight foot terra cotta bas-relief by Henry Kreis, fabricated by Gladding, McBean, depicting the first flag-raising at Fort Moore.

An Early History of Redevelopment

As demographics changed throughout the early twentieth century, Bunker Hill took on a tired, shabby air. The idea of razing the Hill had been floated by the Bunker Hill Razing and Regrading Association as early as 1912, when the Hill was denounced as a barrier between the business center of downtown and the burgeoning neighborhoods of Hollywood and other points west. Plans for redeveloping the Hill began with discussion about boring tunnels through First and Second Streets. The Third Street tunnel, opened in 1901, had been a promising start, but there was a great desire to get traffic passing from the west into the city north of Fifth Street. This led to the formation of the Bunker Hill Razing and Regrading Committee, whose members argued vociferously that the only expedient, worthwhile, and thoughtful expense would be to raze the Hill down to a 3% grade. This had been done, they argued, at Denny Hill in Seattle and Goldsmith Hill in Portland, through hydraulicking, *i.e.*, high-pressure jets of water used to remove rock and sediment. Studies were conducted, and ultimately the City found the $12 million price tag for leveling Bunker Hill unpalatable. A 1913 editorial in the *Los Angeles Times* posited that the area, once razed, would make a fine Central Park on par with Manhattan's, a fitting accompaniment for the burgeoning municipal and federal buildings, anchored by a great library. Instead, the city council elected to construct two tunnels, at Second and First Streets.

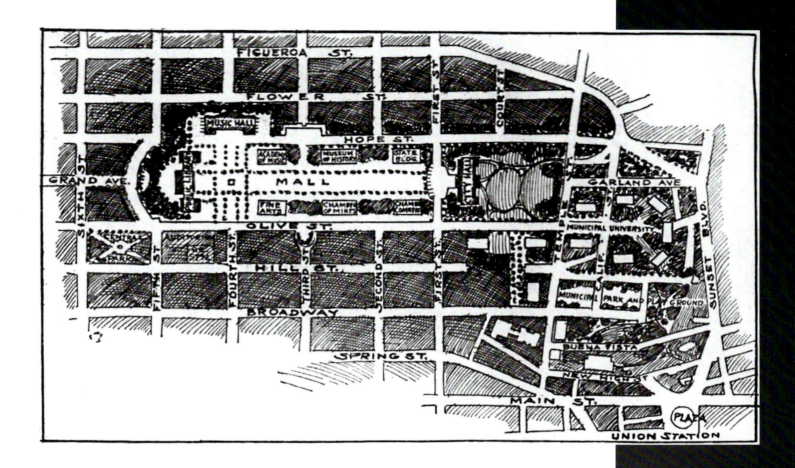

(Though it took another twelve years to finally bore the Second Street tunnel through the Hill; it finally opened in 1924.)

By 1915, a new group formed among local property owners, the Bunker Hill Open Cut Association, which advocated for a wide cut through the Hill, 888 feet across, to form a great avenue from Hill Street to Figueroa. The idea for the cut died in April 1916, after citizens gave it the thumbs-down in a straw poll, which caused the City's assessment department to realize that the majority of the district opposed slicing through their homes. Nevertheless, Bunker Hill was still spoken of as "the real menace to the city's proper development and the chief contributing cause of our street congestion."

In January 1925, at the request of city and county authorities, Allied Architects Association—designers of the Hall of Justice at Temple Street and Broadway—produced a plan for demolishing Bunker Hill and Fort Moore Hill and transforming them into a park and mall, flanked by large courthouses and a variety of city and federal buildings. An illustration by *Los Angeles Times* staff artist Charles H. Owens shows the majority of Bunker Hill as a mile-long park stretching north from the Central Library at Hope and Fifth Streets, which was then under construction.

Probably the greatest and most fully realized prewar redevelopment proposal for Bunker Hill was drafted by Lloyd Wright, son of Frank Lloyd Wright, in 1925. Wright's project has all the hallmarks of

The "Marble Vision of Bunker Hill"—a plan to erect a "double row of civic palaces"—according to the Civic Planning Association, "to build on this a great library, music hall, auditorium, City Hall, fine arts building, museum of science and history, a great municipal or Southern California State University...." 1917.

Essence of Sunshine and Noir

The plan by Allied Architects included a monumental promenade along the top of Bunker Hill. December 1924.

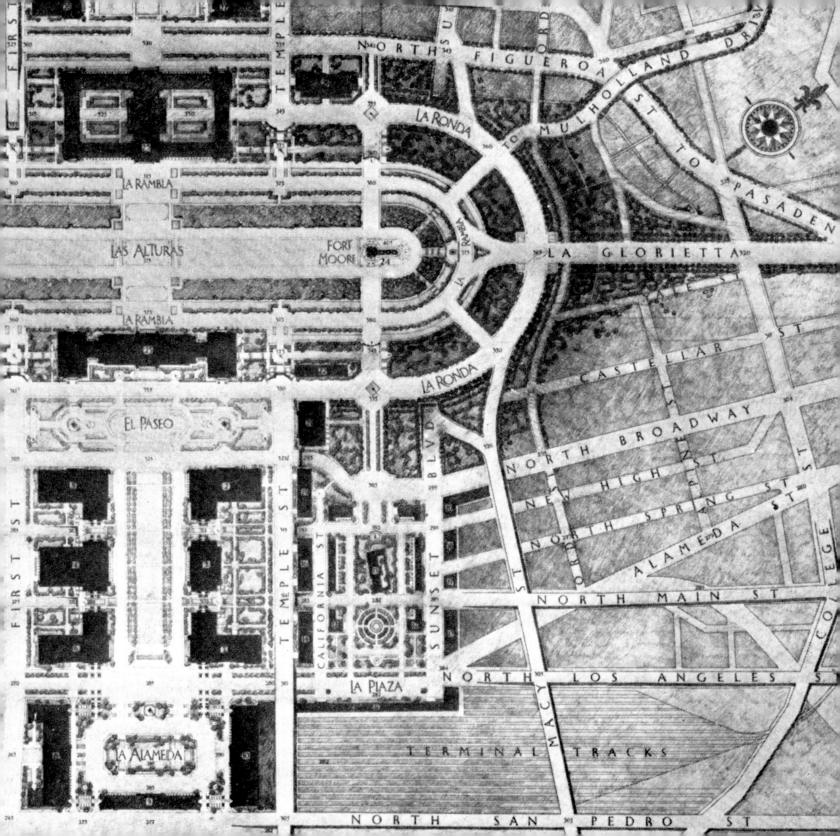

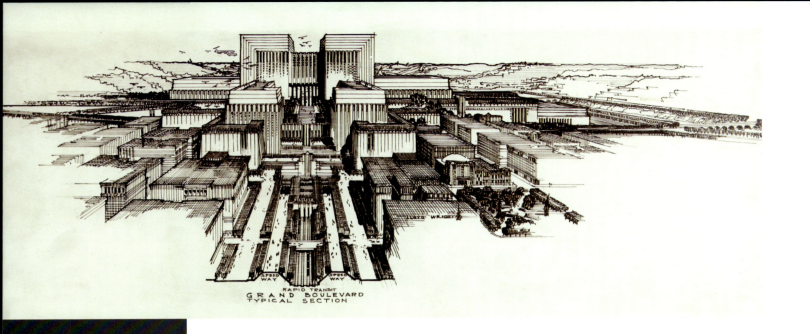

Lloyd Wright's vision: replace Bunker Hill with colossal concrete towers. This plan looks north from Central Library between Olive and Flower Streets. 1925.

1920s technological utopianism—the elimination of grade crossings through the elevated separation of train, auto, and pedestrian traffic, and the inclusion of urban airplane landing strips, which were *de rigueur* in visionary urbanism, as often seen in the renderings of architectural delineators Hugh Ferriss and Harvey Wiley Corbett. Said Wright of his Bunker Hill scheme, it would be "a civic center more magnificent than the hanging gardens of Babylon, enriched with an indigenous and individual architecture and a unity of physical organization more nobly beautiful than has yet been conceived by man."

By "indigenous," Wright was likely referring to the idea that the monumental setback style was the correct and true Western building type due to the stepped forms of the pre-Hispanic ziggurat; this idea, that the setback-style skyscraper was indigenous to the Americas, was further set forth by architect and theorist Francisco Mujica, who in the late 1920s asserted that, via pre-Columbian pyramid architecture, the stepped form was part of a "native" visual language. Wright's father's influence is to be seen as well, given that his Mayan Revival block houses had been designed in the years previous, and under Lloyd's direction. Wright's grandiose plans of the 1920s, like those created by Ferriss and Corbett, fell victim to the Depression, and visionary urbanism was co-opted by the buoyant, optimistic, consumerist World's Fairs of the 1930s, whose "City of the Future" dioramas were less about promulgating utopianism and more about selling streamlined toasters.

The idea of redeveloping the Hill was stirred up again in Spring 1928. Clarence C. Bigelow, of the Southwestern Investment Corporation, conceived of a proposal to demolish the Hill using hydraulic mining equipment. This would not only free traffic movement, but also increase property values after the removal of twenty million cubic yards of earth. Bigelow had a $25,000,000 pledge underwritten by an Eastern bonding house for the project. The Downtown Merchants' Association and the Los Angeles Commercial Board jumped on the plan with alacrity. The city council was ready to appropriate $10,000 for an economic and engineering study to determine feasibility of regrading, when the stock market crashed in 1929. That should have ended the idea, but Henry Babcock, of William Babcock & Sons, a firm of real estate valuators and consultants, arrived from Chicago and took it upon himself to study the feasibility of the Bigelow Plan, and became its tireless proponent.

Bunker Hill, Los Angeles

Said one critic, a David K. Edwards, in a letter to the *Los Angeles Times* in June 1930:

> I have no confidence in the satisfactory outcome of so destructive a proposition as the wrecking of thousands of buildings, miles of streets and sidewalks, sewer, and storm-drain connections, lighting, etc., etc. all of which has been paid for by the property owners, whose properties are now being so depreciated by the hanging over them of this Bigelow project.

In the 1930s, there was a fundamental shift in the nature of redevelopment plans. Planners were less concerned about the Hill as a traffic barrier to the business district, and more concerned about its reputation as a breeding ground for social ills. President Franklin D. Roosevelt, in an effort to jump-start the economy, set aside America's traditional economic theorist Adam Smith, and adopted John Maynard Keynes's model, believing that the country would spend its way out of the Depression by using government funds for social improvement projects. With the Keynesian model in mind, slum clearance began in 1933 under the Public Works Administration (PWA); it razed more than 10,000 occupied units nationally.

Housing demolition was a cornerstone of the Progressive model: Progressives believed in using the government for social engineering, whereby remaking the physical environment would produce better social behavior. When the courts ruled that the PWA did not have sufficient legal basis to take people's homes, Congress passed the United States Housing Act of 1937, which gave the state greater powers of eminent domain; *i.e.*, the condemnation and appropriation of private property by the government for the "greater good." The 1937 Housing Act was drafted primarily by Catherine Bauer, a public housing advocate. Bauer had trained in Europe under Walter Gropius, André Lurçat and Ernst May. She was awarded a Guggenheim fellowship in 1936 to study housing in the USSR—thus, she brought tactics straight out of the European Modernist playbook when she became the first director of the United States Housing Authority (USHA).

Los Angeles Mayor Frank Shaw had asked the federal government for housing demolition monies, and aid in developing public housing projects, as early as 1934. It was not until after the Housing Act of 1937 that Shaw, with the city council, established a Los Angeles Housing Authority in March 1938. By August, Los Angeles had secured $25,000,000 in federal funds from the USHA for slum clearance and low-cost housing. Shaw, though a Republican, was a staunch supporter of the New Deal, and, in a resolution adopted by the Los Angeles Housing Authority that August, was praised for having "widened understanding of the needs and problems of the underprivileged in the city's population … assuring great benefit to our most unfortunate citizens." By May 1942, 175 acres across Los Angeles were appropriated and cleared, and 3,466 units were constructed across ten public housing projects.

Bunker Hill would seem to be the logical place for redevelopment into public housing—it had a shopworn air that connoted blight, and was a stone's throw from Los Angeles City Hall, creating an embarrassment. But not everyone was so sanguine about the prospect of redeveloping Bunker Hill; George J. Eberle, a statistician for the City who specialized in the reduction of waste and inefficiency, wrote in the 1941 collection of essays on land use patterns *Los Angeles: Preface to a Master Plan*:

> Bunker Hill is not a detriment to the downtown area, it is an asset. It supplies excellent sites for superior types of multiple dwellings commanding a view of the entire surrounding country. Such structures would provide replenishment of the downtown tributary resident purchasing power which is urgently needed, and encourage the rehabilitation of near-by blighted areas.

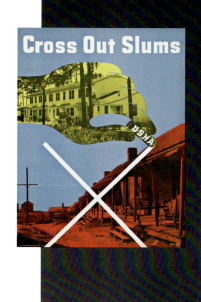

A poster for the United States Housing Authority by modernist designer Lester Beall. The God-like hand of modern housing crosses out the red hell of slum life. 1941.

Essence of Sunshine and Noir

Nevertheless, Mayor Fletcher Bowron, in a 1944 radio address, stated that "something radical, something bold, something new and progressive should be done by making a new section of the city out of an old and blighted area...think of a new apartment house section, with a new park and other improvements, on Bunker Hill!" Bowron's words were prophetic; a great tide was moving in to wipe Bunker Hill clean.

The Hill Casts a Long Shadow: Bunker Hill and Los Angeles Noir

Bunker Hill is often associated with criminality, despair, and all manner of vice and vespertine activity. The Hill was, from its boom in the late 1880s, the target of crime, because of its wealthy residents and hotel patrons. Numerous reports of "sneak-thieves" exist in pre-WWI newspaper accounts of watches and jewelry purloined from hotel rooms. The reprobates of Main Street were but a few blocks below, and these "hoboes" and "yeggs" turned their eye to the pickings above, when a hotel's devious bellboys weren't making off with small fortunes. As the moneyed classes—no strangers to moral turpitude themselves, of course—moved away, they were supplanted by those of humbler birth. As the demographics of the area changed, Bunker Hill became known as a high-crime area. Some generalized that it was because the poor and disenfranchised are predisposed to acts of lawlessness. Others contended that law enforcement would unduly target the people of Bunker Hill, disproportionately harassing the impoverished, the homosexuals, and the bohemians of its diverse community. We might also consider that accounts of crime on the Hill—from the *Los Angeles Times*, city fathers, and the like—were skewed, depicting life there as unhealthy, amid their efforts to provoke support for redevelopment.

Whether or not the actual morality of the Hill's inhabitants was as shabby as the paint on their shutters is not the issue: For those whose initial exposure to Bunker Hill came from mid-century American films noir and interbellum pulp authors, Bunker Hill developed a reputation as a hotbed of corruption and crime.

Fictional Portrayals

Bunker Hill is first seen with warts and scars in the hardboiled style of fiction gaining popularity in the late 1920s. Novelist Don Ryan was the first to portray the Hill in his 1927 book *Angel's Flight*, wherein he treats readers to one of the first depictions of Los Angeles not from the booster's point of view, but as "filled with grotesque cripples," a place of "groaning cable cars" and "barren decrepitude." In 1932 came Paul Cain's *Fast One*, consolidated from a collection of stories Cain had written for *Black Mask*, a pulp magazine specializing in crime, mystery, and detective stories. Now regarded as one of the most hardboiled novels of them all, its protagonist haunts the areas around First and Hill Streets, and Fourth and Grand.

The foremost chronicler of Bunker Hill in all of its beat-up glory was Raymond Chandler. Chandler himself lived on the Hill, moving into the St. Mark at First and Olive Streets with his mother in 1916. In his novella *The King in Yellow*, penned for the March 1938 issue of *Dime Detective*, Chandler described the scene:

> Court Street was old town, wop town, crook town, arty town. It lay across the top of Bunker Hill and you could find anything there from down-at-heels ex-Greenwich-villagers to crooks on the lam, from ladies of anybody's evening to County Relief clients brawling with haggard

landladies in grand old houses with scrolled porches, parquetry floors, and immense sweeping banisters of white oak, mahogany, and Circassian walnut.

It had been a nice place once, had Bunker Hill, and from the days of its niceness there still remained the funny little funicular railway, called the Angel's Flight, which crawled up and down a yellow clay bank from Hill Street.

In 1938, at the time he wrote *King in Yellow*, Chandler and his wife Cissy lived in the Palm Terrace Apartments, at 625 West Fourth St. The Court Street area he mentions in *King in Yellow* was located four blocks north of the Palm Terrace, between Bunker Hill Avenue and Hope Street.

By 1942, Chandler had replaced protagonist Steve Grayce with Philip Marlowe, and reworked his earlier writing into the novel *The High Window* in a passage that has been so widely repeated it has become indelibly associated with the neighborhood:

> Bunker Hill is old town, lost town, shabby town, crook town. Once, very long ago, it was the choice residential district of the city, and there are still standing a few of the jigsaw Gothic mansions with wide porches and walls covered with round-end shingles and full corner bay windows and spindle turrets. They are all rooming houses now, their parquetry floors are scratched and worn through the once glossy finish and the wide sweeping staircases are dark with time and with cheap varnish laid on over generations of dirt. In the tall rooms haggard landladies bicker with shifty tenants. On the wide cool front porches, reaching their cracked shoes into the sun, and staring at nothing, sit the old men with faces like lost battles.
>
> In and around the old houses there are flyblown restaurants and Italian fruit stands and cheap apartment houses and little candy stores where you can buy even nastier things than their candy. And there are ratty hotels where nobody except people named Smith and Jones sign the register and where the night clerk is half watchdog and half pander.
>
> Out of the apartment houses come women who should be young but have faces like stale beer; men with pulled-down hats and quick eyes that look the street over behind the cupped hand that shields the match flame; worn intellectuals with cigarette coughs and no money in the bank; fly cops with granite faces and unwavering eyes; cokies and coke peddlers; people who look like nothing in particular and know it, and once in a while even men

Essence of Sunshine and Noir

Looking across the corner of Fourth and Hope Streets: the Gibson Apartments, 635 West Fourth St.; the Palm Terrace, 625 West Fourth St.; and the Crestholme, 621 West Fourth St. Circa 1907.

▲▲ **Raymond Chandler's first home on Bunker Hill. Built at 100 South Olive St. in 1903, the Hotel Cecil was originally leased by prominent Jewish businessmen, and was dubbed Bunker Hill's "family hotel for Jews." The Cecil became the St. Mark in 1908, and the Hotel Gladden in 1920. April 1957.**

that actually go to work. But they come out early, when the wide cracked sidewalks are empty and still have dew on them.

Film had an even greater influence than the written word. Prewar filming on the Hill was largely comedic. Charlie Chaplin engaged in fisticuffs at the intersection of Fourth Street and Grand Avenue in his first motion picture, 1914's *Making a Living*. Because Hal Roach's Rolin Film Company (cofounded by Roach in 1914) was headquartered in the Bradbury mansion at Court and Hill Streets, hundreds of short comedies featuring Harold Lloyd, Snub Pollard, Bebe Daniels, and others were shot around the Hill.

During and after World War II came a new style of motion picture: film noir. Noir was born from the development of smaller cameras, an influx of European refugee filmmakers, and a prevalence of "B" pictures. A world awash in bloody conflict produced disillusionment that expressed itself in noir's familiar tropes: a fascination with guilty men, damaged women, and dark streets. People know Bunker Hill was torn down, with the understanding that it was decaying and destitute and beyond reclamation architecturally, but through film noir we learn that it was beyond redemption morally.

Studios often elected to film on location, rather than on the backlot, because location shooting oozed authenticity. It imparted elemental realism necessary to films purporting to reveal the truth. (Or, in the case of, say, Roger Corman shooting *Little Shop of Horrors*, Bunker Hill was where you could shoot without permits because the elderly and immigrant population would turn a blind eye.) A *Los Angeles Times* review of the 1951 Dick Powell picture *Cry Danger* called out Bunker Hill in particular; titled "Los Angeles Setting for Hard-Boiled Drama," the article notes "Powell's Los Angeles is peopled with cagey characters who hang around Bunker Hill, in trailer camps, bars, and bookie joints. They are all out for a fast buck." *Cry Danger* made great use of the New Grand Hotel at 257 South Grand Ave. and staged its climactic shoot-out on Third and Olive Streets.

Dozens of motion pictures feature the Hill in all its moody glory. A few of the most notable Bunker Hill appearances in postwar noir pictures include Ralph Meeker driving under Angels Flight in *Kiss Me Deadly* (1955), Van Heflin's mad descent into the Hill in *Act of Violence* (1949), Gordon MacRae running out of the Fremont Hotel in *Backfire* (1950), and the bank heist plot hatched in the Sunshine Apartments in *Criss Cross* (1949).

Bunker Hill would also provide the appropriately disreputable backdrop for police orientation and training films about prostitution, drug addiction, and other societal maladies. In 1951's *Subject: Narcot-*

Bunker Hill, Los Angeles

Director Douglas Sirk prepares a shot with Patricia Knight and Cornell Wilde in *Shockproof* (1949). The structure in the background, 512 West Second St., is seen in movies as early as 1934 (*Fog Over Frisco*) and as late as 1962 (*Days of Wine and Roses*).

◀◀ Director Edward F. Cline shoots a scene for Buster Keaton's *Three Ages* atop the Hill Street Tunnel. 1923.

◀◀◀ Edith Roberts and Earl Hughes are menaced by Margaret Livingston inside the Bradbury Mansion in Andrew L. Stone's first feature film, *Dreary House* (1928).

◀◀◀◀ David Wayne portrayed the child murderer in the 1951 remake of *M*. It cleverly replaced the dark alleyways of Weimar Berlin with the sunlit seediness of postwar Los Angeles, utilizing numerous Bunker Hill locations.

ics, by the renowned Denis and Terry Sanders, a dope addict and his pusher get busted by undercover detectives who roll up on them in front of the Chestmere Apartments, at the northeast corner of Court Street and Grand Avenue; at the end of the film, a junkie wanders Olive Street and down Fourth toward Hill Street, as the narrator intones he is headed "back to the desperate race of men." In 1958's *The Narcotics Story*, a police training film that saw theatrical release, a team of LAPD officers stakes out and finally tackles a heroin dealer at the Ems Hotel, 321 South Olive St., and a young lady in the throes of addiction turns to prostitution at the May Hotel, 209 South Olive St.

Vice and Crime

There was no small quantity of vice on the Hill, either. In 1904, police raided a notorious madam, Ethel Wood, at 355 South Hill St. They arrested her and her three girls were "vagged," that is, charged with vagrancy, the accepted charge for prostitutes until the term of "offering" came into vogue. Raids through 1904 closed the "notorious parlor houses and other places of rendezvous for the members of the half-world."

Essence of Sunshine and Noir

After the November 1914 enactment of the Red Light Abatement Act—passed by the State Legislature in an effort to eliminate brothels—Los Angeles's first raid involved men from the district attorney's office and the Metropolitan Squad descending on the Hotel Clayton, 310 South Clay St. (formerly the Hotel Lorraine). The cops nabbed ten men and seven women, including proprietress Mrs. Florence Cheney. She was held on $5000 bail for pandering and $2000 bail for contributing to the delinquency of her underage granddaughter. Many Joneses and Smiths were loaded, sans trousers, into the paddy wagon. The Stanford rooming house at 360 South Hill would be closed under the act in 1917, but the New Broadway Hotel at 201–215 North Broadway was Los Angeles's worst. There were thirty-five arrests between October 1921 and June 1923, primarily for violations of the Red Light Act. District Attorney Asa Keyes asserted that the New Broadway had "a general reputation in the community as a house of ill-fame and a place where prostitution is encouraged and allowed," as well as numerous Prohibition violations.

Folks were arrested for deviance. It was October 1941, and newlyweds Elizabeth and Richard Nunes lived in the Orth Apartments, at 125 North Grand Ave. They had met at a carnival and, after keeping company for a couple years, eloped to Nevada. Elizabeth, eighteen, was heartbroken to learn that Richard, twenty-five, was in fact Frances, a girl who had passed for a boy for fourteen years. (*Reportedly* heartbroken, that is—later, more LGBTQ-friendly accounts detail that the bride knew Richard was not a man.) Indeed, Frances Orlando, daughter of a wealthy Los Gatos rancher, had been arrested for being transgender many times since 1926. Genuinely astounded, the Studio Carpenter's Union posted her bail, as she was one of its best craftsmen. Frances was acquitted of the charge of False Personation.

Whether or not writers and filmmakers exaggerated the darker element of Bunker Hill, crime did exist on its slopes. Of course, to our contemporary eye, the vice and criminality on the Hill might appear tepid. In a 1956 *Los Angeles Times* article headlined "Bunker Hill Pictured as Crime Haunt," Community Redevelopment Agency (CRA) chairman William T. Sesnon Jr., decrying the Hill's density, claimed, "There is little opportunity for young people to improve their standard of living under these conditions, and it is believed that this is a contributory factor in the high frequency of vice offenses in this area." The article goes on to describe an LAPD report filed with the CRA, which stated:

> Narcotic peddlers, addicts, prostitutes, and thieves of various classifications are common in the area, the police declare. The police report also described Bunker Hill as a secondary Skid Row, with bars along Hill St. and W. 3rd St. notorious as hangouts for undesirables.

The "secondary Skid Row" of West Third Street. Above, the backs of the better homes that lined South Bunker Hill Avenue. 1963.

59

Newsmen and detectives descend on Alvarez & Moore for the surrender of Winnie Ruth Judd. October 23, 1931.

▲▲ **A man encounters trash-picking vagrants near the Angels Flight trestle on Clay Street. Circa 1959.**

The report disclosed that the incidence of juvenile delinquency per 1,000 children was 31.6 as compared with a 7.88 average in the county. Similarly, according to a 1959 CRA report, the average crime rate per 1,000 people in Los Angeles was 43, while for Bunker Hill it was 88; the average city arrest rate per 1,000 was 71, while on the Hill it was 618.

Much of the crime on the Hill was of the routine bar-fight variety. Just as the *Times* had mentioned in its 1956 article, the area along Third Street from the west portal of the tunnel below Hope Street to Figueroa Street was the "secondary skid row," no stranger to pawn shops, liquor stores, bars, and cheap rooms. Again, to our modern eye it may appear perfectly vibrant; given its dearth of boarded-up storefronts and tent cities, it stands in marked contrast with what we today would deem "skid row." Still, it did not lack for drunken brawls ending in tragedy; gents stepping outside of Lou's Cafe, 728 West Third St., resulted in the beating death of one of the combatants in May 1943 and again in September 1944; an argument resulted in the death of a bar patron on the pavement outside Jack's Cafe, 731 West Third St., in April 1944; Sam's Bowery, 833 West Third St., was where one bar patron pushed another, fatally, head first onto the concrete floor in July 1956; and so on.

One of the more striking events in Bunker Hill's annals of odd affairs occurred October 23, 1931. Winnie Ruth Judd, a medical secretary in Phoenix, decided she could win a gentleman's affections by murdering two of her girlfriends, chopping up their bodies, packing their dismembered parts into trunks, and traveling with the trunks to Los Angeles. She aroused suspicion upon arriving in Los Angeles, as the trunks were leaking fluid, so Winnie fled into the city on foot and was, for five days, the most-wanted woman in America. When at last convinced by her husband to surrender, she was picked up at the Biltmore Garage at Fifth Street and Grand Avenue, and taken to the Alvarez & Moore Mortuary at the southwest corner of Olive and Court Streets, where police took her into custody. (The attorney Judd's husband hired, Louis P. Russill, was a friend of mortician Gus Alvarez, which made the mortuary a friendly spot to surrender.) Committed to an asylum for the insane, she escaped many times, including one prolonged absence when she worked as a maid for a wealthy family for six years before her recapture. She was paroled and released in 1971.

The Hill also had its fair share of suicides. There's a "chicken or the egg" element to investigating the topic: Were the desperate naturally attracted to the Hill, or did living on the Hill breed desperation? The Belmont Hotel, at 251 South Hill St. was unusually enticing to the despondent, and was particularly attractive to men in the throes of divorce, or young ladies in failing health, who periodically flung themselves from ledges and out windows.

It does not seem there were greater or fewer murders on the Hill than occurred elsewhere across Los Angeles. The first high-profile killing to make the papers was rich kid Martin Cahen, beaten for his valuables and dying of his injuries, behind the Ems Hotel at 321 South Olive St. in December 1910, and from there, some three dozen acts of big-city violence befell Bunker Hill. There was no dearth of spurned lovers, like Bruce Moore, who murdered Harriet Allen in the Alta Vista at Third Street and Bunker Hill Avenue in 1933.

Redevelopment Takes Hold

Los Angeles faced a housing crisis after World War II, largely due to the great influx of workers who had arrived in the Southland to labor in defense industries. The California Housing Authority determined that ten thousand new units were needed to house the growing population, while at the same time, eviction notices were being served for those in the path of the coming Hollywood Freeway.

In July 1945, the California Legislature, backed by labor unions and housing lobbyists, enacted the Community Redevelopment Act. Though opposed by the Los Angeles Chamber of Commerce on ideological grounds, the Act gave Los Angeles the authority to establish a redevelopment agency to clear blight however defined, whether containing slums or simply having a low-income tax base. The city council declared the need for a redevelopment agency in April 1948, and that October, Mayor Fletcher Bowron appointed the first five commissioners of the Los Angeles Community Redevelopment Agency (CRA). It would be the CRA's job to identify slums to be redeveloped, to condemn and take the property through eminent domain, hold public hearings, and accept Federal funding for demolition. July 1949 saw the passage of the Taft-Ellender-Wagner Act, better known as the American Housing Act of 1949. Like previous housing acts, the 1949 Housing Act empowered the government to seize property by eminent domain to build public housing, but what made this act different was its Title I, which uncoupled the taking of private property specifically from the building of public housing. Bunker Hill would have been, in theory, no different from any other mass Los Angeles taking via eminent domain. Los Angeles had had a policy of slum clearance equivalent elimination since March 1941. The City had seized and cleared 173 acres under the 1937 Housing Act to build 3,468 units in 1941–1942. Public housing had continued apace through the early 1950s, under the 1949 Housing Act—clearing 277 acres to build 4,357 units and depopulating Chavez Ravine—before the federal housing contract was canceled by the City in 1953.

And yet Bunker Hill would be different: Title I of the 1949 Act, by allowing residential/commercial/industrial to be built when slums were cleared, and through the involvement of public/private

Clothes hang out to dry behind the Castle, 325 South Bunker Hill Ave. December 1961.

partnerships, abjured the public housing angle. As a result, the usual consortium of bulldozer-wielding housing developers—the labor unions and left-wing civic groups—would gradually diminish in power. Rather, it was bankers and businessmen, more concerned with stabilizing land values than with reversing social ills, who would come to act as the primary driver of redevelopment.

On September 20, 1949, the CRA examined a slate of ten blighted areas, and chose Bunker Hill as their initial venture, naming it Central Redevelopment Area One. Said Mayor Bowron:

> We have an opportunity here to make Los Angeles a better city in which to live. To maintain an attractive and economically sound city, it is essential that we eliminate the slums and redevelop the blighted areas to the best social and economic use. The selection of Bunker Hill as the first target is a vigorous start on a program of great importance to every citizen.

Voters were asked to go to the polls and authorize a $5 million revolving bond to help cover costs of funding the purchase and clearance of property on Bunker Hill, in the form of Proposition C, placed on the municipal primary ballot on April 3, 1951. A resolution adopted by the Bunker Hill Property Owners Association read: "The adoption of C will mean a tremendous amount of loss, grief,

and trouble to the owners of property on Bunker Hill. The only crime of which our people can be safely charged is hanging clothes to dry in a backyard."

Henry A. Babcock, who had worked to push through the Bigelow Plan for razing Bunker Hill in the early 1930s, was the consulting engineer on Proposition C. Babcock's plan for Bunker Hill involved thirty-seven thirteen-story towers on seventy-three acres, with four 600-car parking garages, open paved lots for 2,560 autos, and 44,000 square feet of retail at its center. The *Los Angeles Times* reported in April 1951:

> Babcock yesterday completed and turned over to the city's Community Redevelopment Agency tentative plans for the apartment buildings which, he said, "are not of the luxury-type apartment found on San Francisco's Nob Hill, but, rather, are designed for the working man and woman. Rents will be easily within their reach."

Opponents were real estate concerns, homeowners, and the patriotic set, who maintained that the taking of private property was contrary to Americanism. Also opposed was G.E. Morris, general head of the Department of Building and Safety, who held that if the City and city council got behind rehabilitation through code enforcement, the issue of blight would be resolved without redevelopment. However, Mayor Bowron, siding with labor unions and assorted religious, civic, and left-liberal organizations, was in favor of Babcock's plan.

Proposition C failed: Investors were disinterested in Bunker Hill. The CRA reduced its staff from seven to three. With the defeat of Proposition C, and the resulting lack of funding, it would be safe to assume that Bunker Hill would be spared from redevelopment. The CRA was, however, reinvigorated by the passage of Proposition 18 in November 1952. Proposition 18 proposed tax increment financing: it permitted the earmarking of increased tax revenue from new development for the retirement of debt incurred by the CRA, potentially bypassing federal aid or bond issues for financing. Those who voted for Proposition 18, on the assertion in the *Los Angeles Times* that it would free the CRA from "federal domination" and "federal bureaucracy," may have been dismayed when the agency proceeded to apply for federal aid at every opportunity.

In November 1954, the city council authorized the CRA to request $33 million from the Housing and Home Finance Agency with which to purchase, clear, and redesign Bunker Hill. Of this, only $250,000 was earmarked for the relocation of the area's residents. There were those who mustered opposition against redevelopment. The Downtown Community Association (DCA) organized to use Title I money to rehabilitate existing housing on the Hill. The Apartment Association of Los Angeles County, Home Builders Institute, and Los Angeles Realty Board rallied alongside the DCA. Property owners also submitted alternative development plans, which intended to utilize Federal Housing Authority loans to rehabilitate the Hill, in accordance with the Housing Act of 1954. These contrary interests, however, especially property owners, did not have the luxury of expensive feasibility studies, or architects and planners, with untold sums subsidized by the federal government, to sway the city council during hearings.

One such property owner with an alternative development plan was influential civic figure and

A model depicts the redevelopment of Bunker Hill. The round structure bounded by Fifth, Figueroa, Fourth, and Flower Streets was to be a Los Angeles Memorial Auditorium designed by William Pereira. The redevelopment and a proposed Music Center overlooking Lafayette Park failed to be funded in a 1951 bond issue. 1950.

Essence of Sunshine and Noir

Architect Charles Luckman presents plans for the Bunker Hill project to councilman John S. Gibson and CRA chairman William T. Sesnon Jr. November 1955.

▲▲ Stuart K. Oliver poses with his modern house, 351 South Hope St. December 1954.

residential developer Fritz Bernard Burns, past president of the Home Builders Association of Los Angeles and of the National Association of Home Builders. Said Burns in April 1955, "It is not in the best interest of the people and a waste of taxpayer's money to tear down hundreds of good old houses to eliminate a comparative handful of unsalvageable ones unless you want to establish the precedent of tearing down all buildings fifty years old or older." Burns had made a point of buying and rehabilitating old properties on the Hill.

Not only were the houses on the Hill worth being restored and refurbished, but it also was disingenuous to assert that all Bunker Hill was ancient and archaic. Its southern flank along Fifth Street contained many art deco structures. Within Bunker Hill proper, there were Streamline Moderne storefronts like the Angels Flight Café, Late Moderne design to be seen on the Grand Avenue Telephone Building, and, most notably, there was the house of Stuart K. Oliver, who in 1951 decided to build his modern home high atop Fourth and Hope Streets, overlooking the city below.

Bunker Hill was modern in other ways, as well. Its relationship with and response to the automobile is especially noteworthy. The three Hill Street tunnels, the Broadway tunnel, and the First Street and Second Street tunnels were major civic improvements. The Subway Terminal on Hill Street, whisking people back and forth from below Bunker Hill, was a technological marvel. As the car began to dominate Los Angeles in the early 1920s, the area around Fourth and Olive Streets sprouted garages by major architects—including Curlett & Beelman's Savoy Auto Park at 400 South Olive Street, which still stands and is today the oldest parking garage in Los Angeles. One block south at Fifth Street and Grand Avenue, the Grand Central Garage was, at the time of its completion in 1920, the largest garage in the world.

But ultimately Bunker Hill was distinguished by its Queen Anne architecture, and anything Victorian took on an increasingly unsavory air over time, more than just connoting bad taste. Polygonal towers and stained glass represented a bloated, death-obsessed time, a Gilded Age seen after World War I as a vile and corrupt era. Artist Charles Burchfield depicted Victorian architecture as ominous and possibly menacing in his 1924 painting *House of Mystery*, as did Edward Hopper in his *House by the Railroad* (1925). Novelist Alexander Laing, writing about an uncanny house of horrors in *The Cadaver of Gideon Wyck* (1933), said, "Obviously, nothing could have been done about the house without razing it and building anew … they had left it just as they found it: a monument to the most tasteless period of American Victorianism." Over the coming years, vintage architecture took on a sillier, less sinister aura in popular culture, for example, the Victorian home of comedic murderous spinsters in 1941's *Arsenic*

Bunker Hill, Los Angeles

and Old Lace, or Charles Addams's Addams Family in the *New Yorker* cartoons, living together in their gleefully ghoulish, mansard-roofed house.

Through the 1950s, while property owners and the CRA battled over the 136 acres of Bunker Hill south of First Street, the Hill was being eaten away by various other projects outside the purview of the CRA. There of course had been demolition of houses over the years. Fourth Street, which ended at Flower Street, was widened in 1954 during construction of the "Fourth Street Cut," a 32-foot-deep, 687-foot-long viaduct resulting in the loss of many prominent buildings, including the Fremont Hotel, Hildreth mansion, and the Castle Towers Apartments. Another major traffic artery, the Hollywood Freeway, took out much of adjacent Fort Moore Hill to the north.

The area north of First Street, bounded by First, Hill, Court, and Olive Streets, was depopulated and leveled by the Los Angeles City Housing Authority, which removed more than two thousand people between mid-1949 and July 1950, demolishing fifty-seven residences and nineteen commercial structures, ultimately clearing 639 units for the proposed Department of Water and Power offices. This area, however, was subsequently purchased by the Los Angeles County Board of Supervisors in July 1953 along with the rest of the area bounded by First, Hill, Temple Streets and Grand Avenue, to become the site of the new courthouse; its foundation was poured in the summer of 1954.

The six-story Los Angeles County Courthouse, designed by an architectural consortium comprised of Jesse E. Stanton, Paul R. Williams, Adrian Wilson, and the firm of Austin, Field, and Fry, was dedicated by Chief Justice Earl Warren in October 1958. The Hall of Administration opened in October 1960. The blocks to the south, bounded by Second, Hill, Hope, and First Streets—which held the Melrose Hotel and the Berke mansion—were taken by the County in 1957 to build surface parking lots for the burgeoning civic center. The County Courthouse and Hall of Administration also required the removal of the iconic twin bore Hill Street tunnels, as well as the very hill that contained them.

It was time, at last, for Bunker Hill to become the civic and cultural acropolis promoted with such visionary vigor in the 1920s. For decades, the Los Angeles Philharmonic had performed in space rented from the Temple Baptist Church at Fifth and Olive Streets. Three early-1950s bond measures to fund a performing arts center downtown all failed. It required the leadership of Dorothy Buffum Chandler, who had rescued the Hollywood Bowl from bankruptcy in 1951, to establish a public-private partnership that would bring the Music Center to life. Chandler proposed to the County, in 1955, that she build her hall with private funds on County lands leased for one dollar a year. Money was raised,

As the Courthouse skeleton rose in June 1956, the *Los Angeles Times* rhapsodized, "Los Angeles is creating a work of art in its new Civic Center. Its brushes are steel and concrete, bulldozers and power shovels." 1960.

▲▲ **The 1952 City Planning Commission model showing the various proposed structures (in white) amongst the city, county, state and federal buildings that comprised the Civic Center.**

Essence of Sunshine and Noir

▼▼ **Looking west across the Music Center Plaza toward the Pavilion, before the addition of Jacques Lipchitz's sculpture *Peace on Earth* at the center of the fountains. February 1965.**

A view of the Department of Water and Power, looking east from Huntley Drive. December 1965.

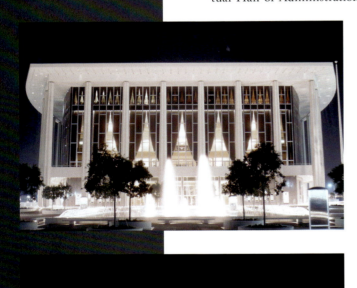

leaseback arrangements were legalized, and by early 1960 the firm of Welton Becket & Associates was engaged to design the site. The grandeur and serenity of the center's acropolis setting gave Becket the freedom to indulge a New Formalist aesthetic, giving it an overhanging roof like a classical cornice, and a portico of stylized fluted columns surrounding a black granite and tinted glass façade. Construction began in March 1962, west of the Courthouse and Hall of Administration, on what was called "The Music Center, a Living Memorial to Peace," which included the 3,200-seat Memorial Pavilion, the 1,800-seat Center Theatre, and the 800-seat Forum for drama and chamber music. Mrs. Chandler initially set out to raise $4 million; she raised $18.7 million, by vigorously campaigning among old and new money alike—oil men, entertainment folk, scions of industry. Two of the earliest and most significant donations came from American Savings and Loan's Mark Taper, and Home Savings and Loan's Howard Ahmanson. The Music Center was dedicated in December 1964, and Chandler made the cover of *Time* magazine. In December 1965, the County Board of Supervisors voted to name the three buildings after those who had made the most major contributions: the Memorial Pavilion thus became the Dorothy Chandler Pavilion, the Forum became the Mark Taper Forum, and the Center Theatre became the Ahmanson Theatre.

Bunker Hill became the home for another major work of architectural art on county-held land. The Department of Water and Power began acquiring land west of the burgeoning civic center for its headquarters in the 1930s. After selling those lands along Hill Street to the County for its eventual Hall of Administration and County Courthouse, the DWP board in 1955 selected a different site bounded by Temple, First, Hope, and Figueroa Streets, at the western terminus of the civic center project. The Board of Water and Power Commission hired Albert C. Martin & Associates in 1959 for its general office building. Construction began in January 1962, and the building was dedicated in June 1965. The sixteen-acre grounds were designed by the landscape architecture firm Cornell, Bridgers, and Troller and included, at its northeast corner, giant boulders from the Owens Valley, where Los Angeles sources much of its water. The seventeen-story building, encircled by a reflecting pool, is a landmark of Corporate International architecture. The cantilevered canopies act as solar shades for the full-height bands of windows on each floor. The ceiling system captures heat from its lighting, whereby keeping the lights on is energy efficient, and the fountains in its reflecting pool provide the building's air conditioning via circulating water. Its double-height marble lobby is known for its spiral staircase above a reflecting pool.

Back on the other side of the civic center expansion, the CRA's plan for Bunker Hill continued apace. Hearings were held; representatives of city government, and groups such as the Jewish Labor Council, pressed city council to reject all alternative plans. Attorney Phill Silver made counter arguments against the CRA plan on legal and moral grounds. In November 1956, after months of public hearings, the city council approved the CRA's Tentative Plan, which outlined the intricacies of property acquisition, demolition, and redevelopment construction. Architects outlined proposals, showing a lowered and regraded hill, with

Bunker Hill, Los Angeles

streets closed and realigned to form "superblocks" where major commercial and residential plazas could be grouped. Twenty-nine blocks would be reduced to twenty-three, and streets like Bunker Hill Avenue, Cinnabar Street, Olive Court, and more would simply be absorbed. The superblocks segregated areas by use, and thus dismantled the Hill's intricate interplay of commercial and residential districts. The idea of neighborhoods being compact, walkable, and mixed-use would not become a hallmark of "New Urbanism" for another thirty years. More hearings ensued, and ultimately the City's desire to turn a tax liability into a tax asset won out.

On March 31, 1959, Los Angeles City Council adopted, by a vote of 12 to 2, Los Angeles City Ordinance 113231, approving the Bunker Hill Urban Renewal Project 1-B Plan. The two opponents were the council's most liberal and most conservative members: Councilman Edward R. Roybal objected to CRA's inadequate relocation provisions, and Councilman John C. Holland was concerned about property owners' rights.

With Los Angeles City Council's 1959 acceptance of the CRA's plan for the redevelopment of Bunker Hill, decades of demolition schemes finally came to pass.

Essence of Sunshine and Noir

Architects' drawings, prepared by Pereira & Luckman, Welton Becket & Associates, and Donald R. Warren Co., as presented by the CRA to the mayor, city council, and other top city officials, at the Statler Hotel. February 29, 1956.

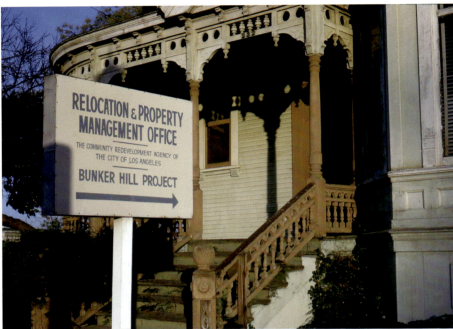

It was on this porch that CRA chairman William T. Sesnon Jr. delivered a check for $68,500 and received title to three pieces of property, May 4, 1961. With that, after more than a decade of planning, the CRA was in the real estate business. May 1957.

▲▲ The house of Bernhard Sens, 232 South Grand Ave., was built in 1894. In 1929, it became the home of Dr. James Green, who was the physician for the Hill until his death in 1956. March 1968.

The 1960s: Demolition and Re-Birth

After the March 1959 adoption of the final Bunker Hill redevelopment plan, multiple suits were filed in superior court. Twenty-six property owners sought injunctions, but on April 20, 1961, Superior Court Judge Phillip H. Richards released a 108-page decision that upheld the legality of the project. Although there were immediate appeals—cases were moved to the California Supreme Court, where they were fought, and finally all lost, through 1964—the Community Redevelopment Agency wasted no time in purchasing property.

On May 5, 1961, the CRA announced it had reached "a milestone some critics said it would never attain" when Chairman William T. Sesnon Jr. turned over a check and received title to three adjacent properties on the Hill. This was done with some pomp and circumstance, with a photo in the *Los Angeles Times* of Sesnon accepting "deed to ancient property at 244 Bunker Hill Ave." (This was a loose use of the term "ancient," since the house was then about seventy years old.) "Because of its significance as the agency's first purchase, the transaction was ceremoniously recorded on the steps of a fading, though once-elegant, residence." What Sesnon had purchased was Lot 3, in Block K of the Mott Tract, which included 244 and 246 South Bunker Hill Ave., and 245 South Grand Ave.

Two weeks later, with an advance from the Housing and Home Finance Agency—the precursor to the Department of Housing and Urban Development—Sesnon had invested or committed more than $4.6 million in the CRA's land-buying program, having title to thirteen more properties, with another eight in escrow.

Bunker Hill, Los Angeles

In June 1961, the CRA opened an office in the former home of Dr. James Green, at 232 South Grand Ave. Here, employees worked to relocate about nine thousand displaced persons during the redevelopment of the 136-acre section. According to CRA Executive Director Joseph T. Bill, residents would receive at least one month's advance notice before it was time to vacate their homes. The Bunker Hill Citizens' Advisory Relocation Committee assisted the CRA in finding housing for displaced residents. By early 1962, advertisements for flats west of downtown began appearing in the *Los Angeles Times* reading "Pensioners Attention! Residents of Bunker Hill—See these outstanding apts that are available Be wise and relocate NOW."

September 11, 1961, was a watershed moment for the CRA. Crews from Cleveland Wrecking Company began dismantling the Hillcrest at 258 South Olive St. The Hillcrest apartments—originally named the Hill Crest Inn—were built in late 1904/early 1905 by Colonel J.W. Eddy adjacent to Angels Flight, which he had constructed four years earlier. The large frame building, designed by architect Henry A. Cogswell, was a landmark, commanding a perch at Third and Olive Streets. Its removal marked the agency's initial venture into demolition work as part of the Bunker Hill Urban Renewal Project. At the time, the CRA had title to, or agreements to purchase, approximately a quarter of the 136-acre project area. The Hillcrest's fifty tenants, primarily long-term and elderly, were relocated. "With this demolition job," said the CRA's Bill, "the work of tearing down other structures will be accelerated to keep pace with the progress of our relocation program."

Relocating displaced residents, pledged Sesnon in his 1961 *Annual Report to the City Council by the Community Redevelopment Agency*, "will not only greatly improve living conditions, but will also set a model for America." Yet newly elected Mayor Samuel Yorty charged the CRA with mishandling the relocation. Said Yorty in a radio address that December, the project had "given redevelopment a

The Hillcrest was three years old in this image. To its south, the original pavilion of Angels Flight, and a newly opened Elks Lodge. 1908.

▼ The Hillcrest, first of the CRA redevelopment removals, is dismantled. September 1961.

Essence of Sunshine and Noir

Looking west across Fifth Street, shot from a window of the Crocker Citizens Bank Tower at Sixth Street and Grand Avenue. Prominent in the image are the Union Bank Plaza gardens designed by noted landscape architect Garrett Eckbo. November 1969.

▶▶ **Destroyed: Crocker Court, 1983-2017. 2011.**

black eye in the community … other cities have done a much better job in redevelopment, conservation, and rehabilitation than has the City of Los Angeles. The Redevelopment Agency … have moved far too slowly in finding other housing for the people displaced on Bunker Hill."

The CRA had $925,000 in federal grant money with which to relocate the Hill's nine thousand-plus residents. The agency allowed up to $200 per family and $3,000 per business for moving. Critics posited that much of the CRA's grant would be used in its bureaucratic administration and compensation to the fourteen staff members assigned to the task, spread across the CRA and the Citizens Relocation Committee.

A February 1962 *Los Angeles Times* article described how much folks enjoyed being relocated, and pulled no punches when describing the Hill as dotted with "rotting old eyesores," a "tumbledown district," populated by "humanity's tumbleweeds." The *Times* asserted that the newer, cleaner quarters also offered cheaper rent. Yet according to the CRA's *Relocation Progress Report of 1963*, 86% of those who were relocated ended up paying higher rent, and 60% of them were moved to an area within one mile of Bunker Hill.

Critics charged that CRA chairman William T. Sesnon, an oil man, was after the Hill's oil deposits; that the taxpayer-funded government land grab was in collusion with private developers. The owner of the Dome Hotel, Frank Babcock, filed an injunction in superior court against the CRA (the Dome Hotel burned afterward in a mysterious 1964 fire). Critics contended that, ultimately, there would be no takers for the new superblocks.

But in March 1965, the Connecticut General Life Insurance Company purchased one of the superblocks at Bunker Hill's southwestern edge, where the 1929 Monarch Hotel stood at Fifth and Figueroa Streets. With great fanfare, it became home to the forty-two-story Union Bank Square tower—the Hill's first "slum clearance" skyscraper. In an effort to set Los Angeles apart from the dark, walled-in cities of the East Coast, city council had enacted a 130-foot height limit on buildings in 1904. The council amended the limit to 150 feet in 1911, before repealing the law entirely in 1956. At 516 feet, Union Bank was the first to actually surpass City Hall. Union Bank Square was dedicated in November 1966 and opened the following month.

It was an auspicious beginning. However, in 1966, City Administrative Officer Erwin Piper issued a scathing management audit report of the CRA, citing faulty operational control, an absence of clear policy, failing to coordinate with city and county departments, and wasted money. Years of delay since the 1959 city council approval had resulted in too few properties purchased, leading to higher acquisition, overhead, and administrative costs, and loss of tax revenue. The CAO report also pointed out that tenants on Bunker Hill were evacuated from structures perfectly suitable for habitation during the ongoing years of litigation, thus depriving the CRA of hundreds of thousands of dollars in potential rental income. Ultimately, Piper concluded that in the CRA's eighteen years without an audit, the agency had been needlessly myopic in only approaching renewal through the bulldozer. The report was so damaging that it led to the resignation of CRA Chairman William T. Sesnon.

In a September 1962 article about the "fight against civic eyesores," the *Los Angeles Times* wrote of the CRA and its land-clearance program:

> ... since the project was proposed, it has remained, the largest core area blight-clearing and redevelopment plan ever undertaken. The project, despite the sluggish way it has progressed, is—as one planner put it—"dramatic, bold, and full of promise." What will Los Angeles get in place of the blighted, spiritless Bunker Hill community that exists now? By 1968, and probably no later than 1970, when the redevelopment process should be completed, there will be a new, towering skyline blending into the downtown silhouette.

After Union Bank Square tower went up, and then the Bunker Hill Towers apartments in 1968, 90% of Bunker Hill—which comprised 20% of downtown, and the most valuable real estate in the City—still lay vacant.

The renewal efforts remained troubled. After some major buildings were erected in the 1970s, the energy crisis and "double dip" recession of the early 1980s put a damper on new construction. The massive five-parcel, 11.2-acre California Plaza plan from 1979 was delayed due in part to financing issues. The recession of the early 1990s and in 2001 didn't help matters, but sometimes buildings just take longer than expected: After Lillian Disney gave $50 million to build a concert hall in 1987, and Frank Gehry was hired to design it, it took sixteen years before a single note was played. Construction stopped repeatedly through the 1990s so officials could study ways to manage spiraling costs, which had reached nearly $200 million (Los Angeles County, which owns the land, paid $110 million for the parking garage alone). Mayor Riordan supported the 1997 plan to take the job away from Gehry, and Gehry threatened to quit, and after six years and another $100 million, the Walt Disney Concert Hall finally opened in October 2003. Disney Hall is arguably the most striking structure on the Hill, if not the most controversial. Some acclaimed its design as daring and groundbreaking, others likened it to a "shoe box left out in the rain." Notably, parts of its stainless steel surface blinded passersby and heated neighboring apartments to 140 degrees Fahrenheit, and were therefore sandblasted in 2005. Ultimately, however, all agreed the acoustics, designed by Minoru Nagata, were superb.

In the sixty-plus years since the Los Angeles City Council approved redevelopment, Bunker Hill is almost entirely developed; only three major parcels remain. One of the last areas to be developed was once part of the 1980s Grand Promenade development that went only half-built, where the Broad museum was constructed in 2015. The final major new building on a demolished piece of "old Bunker Hill"—if it can be called that—is the Gehry-designed Grand Avenue Project, which required the removal of Charles Bentley's experimental 1969 "Tinkertoy" garage. Bentley's revolutionary concept involved building structures assembled like Erector Sets, designed to be taken apart and reassembled elsewhere when needed. Though the 1,062-car structure was never moved, nor

Essence of Sunshine and Noir

was it relocated when, in 2018, just shy of its fiftieth birthday—a stay longer, historically, than a great many Bunker Hill buildings—it was unceremoniously demolished.

With Bunker Hill now built, what do we have? Los Angeles has been gifted a remarkable collection of Late Modern, Postmodern, and contemporary architecture. The Corporate International style Union Bank tower of 1966 defines its time just as the glass-skinned Bonaventure of 1976 across the street encapsulates its era. Muscular granite-sheathed office towers of the 1980s tell the student of that era as much as a J.C. Newsom does about the 1880s. Museums with honeycomb facades, deconstructivist cathedrals, and ship-sail concert halls speak of a new millennium. Many of these prominent Bunker Hill buildings have reached fifty years old, making them eligible for landmark status. The landmarking of buildings in Los Angeles began with discussion of Bunker Hill, and while the landmarked Hill houses burned and nothing of the old Hill remains, ironically, we can turn an eye to what replaced them. Some are obvious: Union Bank and its stunning 1968 Garett Eckbo-designed gardens; the 1974 Security Pacific Bank and its remarkably preserved lobby; and the iconic Bonaventure, which harbors one of the most sublime interiors in the world.

And yet, just as we saw the progressive demolition (before its wholesale demolition) of Bunker Hill once before, we witness it again: among the losses, the remarkable 1983 Lawrence Halprin-designed atrium and its sculptures inside the Wells Fargo towers were destroyed in 2017; the 1964 landscape design for the Music Center by Cornell, Bridgers, and Troller was removed and the sunken plaza filled in 2018; the 1992 California Plaza Watercourt by WET Design had all its water removed in 2019. Much more demolition is planned for Bunker Hill: the 1974 World Trade Center will see the destruction of its completely intact retail concourse, including its 1000-foot-long bas relief by renowned artist Tony Sheets, and incredibly, movement is afoot to demolish the Late Moderne Courthouse and Hall of Administration.

It is ironic that a place as intriguing as Bunker Hill was given to the bulldozers, only so that we might now worry about the demolition of its contemporary replacement. Maybe that's understandable: Touchstones of the recent past usually garner precious little respect, and arguments for their retention and maintenance fall on deaf ears. Nevertheless, this is the Bunker Hill we have and share, and for the last many decades it has grown and morphed into a quizzical cultural landscape.

Modern-day Bunker Hill is both an open-air museum of modern architecture and sculpture and a part of our shared collective memory. Visiting its present, remembering its past, and preserving it for the future is our honor and duty. ●

▶ Gehry's Walt Disney Concert Hall has become an oft-photographed icon of Los Angeles. 2003.

BUNKER HILL
LOS ANGELES

Old Bunker Hill in its final days, January 1969. By May, Angels Flight was dismantled and carted off for twenty-seven years of storage. The McCoy Block (Morgan and Walls, 1905, with the "Royal Liquor" neon) at Third and Hill Streets and the Hotel Belmont (Arthur B. Benton, 1908) had been demolished for decades when the Flight was returned to a new, alien landscape in 1996.

The Early Years

Bunker Hill's earliest structures were the military breastwork, built in 1847, and adobe houses on the northernmost tip of the Hill, bordering Sonoratown. Los Angeles residents had already built along Bunker Hill's base, at Hill Street; after Beaudry's subdivision, in the late 1860s, developers began to build houses on the Hill itself. Beaudry sold lots for between $100 to $525 on an installment plan, requiring only $15 down and $6 a month for this "Fine, Dry, Airy Location—Splendid Views—Most Elegant Part of the City," as he advertised. Those who braved the daunting climb up the Hill were rewarded with a view to the sea. Intrepid Angelenos purchased lots and built cottages in the Folk Victorian style, based on designs found in the illustrated weeklies and lithographs sold in local dry-goods stores. They irrigated their freshly planted lawns and gardens with water from Beaudry's Los Angeles City Water Company and its newly laid iron pipes. Homebuilders, aided by the 1869 railroad line to the docks in Wilmington, were well-supplied with Douglas Fir from the Pacific Northwest to build their balloon-frame Folk Victorian houses; Carpenter Gothic and Italianate styles were also popular.

Harley Taft House
411 West Fifth St. • 1870
Harley Taft purchased the block bounded by Fifth, Hill, Fourth, and Olive Streets for $9.80 in 1866. He built his home facing St. Vincent's Park (now Pershing Square). Its steep cross gable gives a nod to Carpenter Gothic style; decorative elements along the porch exhibit elements of the Folk vernacular.

*The Jesus Manzo Adobe
412 West Sunset Blvd.
Circa 1865*

Jesus Manzo built his adobe home with walls two feet thick, redwood door frames and window paneling, and carved, fluted porch lintels. It was still occupied by Manzo's descendants when demolished in March 1949.

Essence of Sunshine and Noir

Taft Duplex
449/451 South Hill St. • Circa 1882

◀ The Tafts built this duplex next door to their 1870 home. The hipped-roof structure is Italianate with eave brackets and spindlework porch detailing.

Dr. Joseph Pomeroy Widney House
421 South Hill St. • 1882

▲ The Joseph P. Widney House displays an Italianate influence in its quoins, but the strong front-gabled massing is its dominant feature, common in the early Folk vernacular, intended to echo the pedimented façade of Greek temples.

Robert M. Widney House
417 South Hill St. • 1882

◀ The home of Judge Robert M. Widney, adjacent to Dr. Joseph P. Widney's house. The brothers lived together in a one-story duplex at 227/229 South Hill St. in the 1870s—when they co-founded the University of Southern California—before moving to adjoining houses.

William W. Widney House
430 West Fourth St. • 1879
and Robert M. Widney House
416 South Olive St. • 1883

Realtor William Widney and his brother Robert—who had moved up from Hill Street—built adjoining houses on the southeast corner of Fourth and Olive Streets. The *Los Angeles Herald* described Robert Widney's home as "a handsome residence of thirteen rooms of his own design."

Andrew Wilson Potts House
147 North Hill St. • Circa 1877

▶ The home of A.W. Potts, Los Angeles county clerk, was an archetypal Italianate dwelling: hipped roof, bracketed eaves, and tall, pedimented windows. In 1882, the *Los Angeles Times* described an "elegant social party at the Potts mansion ... the spacious parlors ... filled to overflowing with the elite of the city." Potts sold his house to Lewis Leonard Bradbury in February 1885, and Potts's house was moved to Court Street. Bradbury used the site to erect a twenty-seven-room mansion.

Essence of Sunshine and Noir

Salt Box
339 South Bunker Hill Ave.
Circa 1878

Attorney John W. Stump built the Salt Box around 1878. Named for its Colonial configuration, it consisted of two stories in front and one in back, joined by a pitched roof. Dr. A.G. Cook, who purchased it in October 1882, added the bay, lit by five tall, arched windows, on the south side. Subsequent owners Reuben Baker (1887) or Rudolph Weyse (1892) added the front porch and enlarged the back to two stories, making this a poor example of an actual salt box.

Llewellyn Bixby House
138 North Hill St.
Kysor and Morgan • 1881

◀ Rancher Bixby chose this site for its views of Catalina Island. Sarah Bixby Smith wrote in her memoir *Adobe Days* (1925) "It began as a seven-room cottage …. Every house had a bay window in the projecting end, that being the front parlor…" New owners renamed it the Harmonia Apartments in 1914, and it was demolished for a parking lot in 1953. 1928.

Frank Walker House
129 South Olive St. • 1886

▶ Frank Walker, a contractor and city councilman, built his Eastlake home in the summer of 1886. After his wife Delia died in 1891, he rented it out. 1944.

Brousseau Mansion
238 South Bunker Hill Ave. • 1883
The house is an amalgam of styles: an Italianate tower, Stick wall cladding, and squared bay. Its blocked massing lends an Eastlake feel, and its profusion of spindlework is an early expression of Queen Anne. The Brousseau family had their housewarming party on July 2, 1883, at which guests enjoyed refreshments and dancing. December 1961.

George M. Holton House
227 South Bunker Hill Ave. • 1882
▼ The residence of George Holton, a district attorney and superior court judge, was an example of "gable front and wing" Folk Victorian; its wing was added between 1888 and 1894, with the traditional porch spandrels, intricate balustrade, and gable cutwork. June 1961.

Bunker Hill, Los Angeles

Dr. Johann Carl Zahn House
427 South Hope St. • *1887*

The respectable Zahn family built in Italianate style, with grouped, arched windows and bracketed eaves. In 1912, Zahn's widow Frances replaced the house with a Frank M. Tyler-designed neoclassical apartment building known as the Rubaiyat.

▶ Zahn and his English wife Frances "Fannie" Zahn pose with two young men, likely Lorenzo Paul and Hector, their youngest of five sons. Circa 1890.

The Boom of the Eighties

The Philadelphia Centennial Exhibition of 1876 popularized the work of architect Sir Charles Eastlake, whose idea of "artistic moral purpose" in design changed architecture, and aided the rise of Queen Anne style. At the same exhibition—which was visited by a fifth of the nation's population—the Los Angeles Chamber of Commerce circulated a pamphlet extolling the merits of the southland. In 1885, these trends were united when a fare war developed between the Southern Pacific and Santa Fe railroads and the population of Los Angeles swelled from 11,000 to 80,000. These immigrants were generally well-off, often retired, looking to live amongst the fabled orange groves and take in the curative powers of perpetual sunshine. These immigrants "Americanized" Los Angeles, and soon Anglo-Protestant church spires shot up all over the once-Catholic town. Because Queen Anne was by then considered the correct and appropriate residential building design, Bunker Hill became a showplace of the style. Famous homes like the Crocker, Rose, and Bradbury mansions exhibit all the trademark features of Queen Anne: asymmetrical façades, corner towers, balconies, and stained glass. Though Queen Anne structures may appear antiquated, they had everything previous homes did not—rambling floor plans and hygienic sanitation, in an environment of clean air.

Bunker Hill, Los Angeles

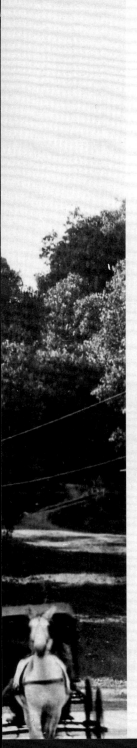

Margaret Crocker Mansion
300 South Olive St.
John Hall • 1886

◄▲ In late 1885, Margaret Eleanor Rhodes Crocker enlisted architect John Hall to design this mix of Stick and Queen Anne styles, sited high above the city at Third and Olive Streets.

Granite came from Devil's Gate quarry near Pasadena, with interior woodwork carved by Henry Bohrmann, the celebrated mantel-maker. Faulty backfill from construction of the Third Street Tunnel caused the house to tilt ten inches, but it nevertheless remained upright. The Elks purchased the Crocker mansion in July 1906 intending to convert it to lodge rooms, but razed it, replacing it with a reinforced concrete structure.

Essence of Sunshine and Noir

Berke Mansion
145 South Bunker Hill Ave. • 1886

Ferdinand Berke arrived during the boom with his wife and four daughters, and began construction on his twenty-room house in August 1886. The mansion became a rooming house known as the Berke in 1898. Pictured here is Berke's eldest daughter Anna.

Berke Mansion, from Hope Street

The Berke was later known as the Warncliffe and, later, the Anderson. With its differentiated towers and mix of gables and dormers, it has all the irregular charm one expects of the 1880s. 1955.

John Alexander Wills Mansion
501 North Broadway
Mary Alston Channing Saunders • 1886
Attorney Wills and family moved into their manse, with close to an acre of gardens, in October 1886. Daughter Madeline Frances—"Fanny"—continued to live in the house, and society pages made note of her lavish mahjong parties, complete with Chinese girls in authentic dress. Fanny was a noted suffragist, and Susan B. Anthony was a frequent houseguest. The County removed her by force in December 1930 and demolished the house six years later.

Essence of Sunshine and Noir

Lewis Leonard Bradbury Mansion
147 North Hill St.
Samuel and Joseph Cather Newsom • 1887

L.L. Bradbury, sea captain and owner of Mexican mines, spent $80,000 on this Newsom-designed mansion for himself and his bride, Simona Martinez. Its exterior was faced with red terra cotta by Gladding, McBean, and its rooms were replete with rare woods. After Bradbury and Simona died, it became a boarding house, the luncheon club for superior court judges, and headquarters for Hal Roach's Rolin Film Company.

▼ The Bradbury's Hill Street façade seen from the top of the courthouse. Circa 1895.

▶ The Court Street frontage of the Mansion. 1928.

Bunker Hill, Los Angeles

Bunker Hill, Los Angeles

The Castle
325 South Bunker Hill Ave. • 1887

The Castle is one of the Hill's best-known lost landmarks. Prior to 1887, there was a cottage on the lot, owned by the Cosett family. Chicago meat-packer Philip Danforth Armour, who owned the Salt Box, had Reuben Moore Baker build the house for him. But Armour left Los Angeles, and Baker moved into the new house in late 1887 or early 1888.

Daniel F. Donegan purchased the house from Baker in 1894; under his stewardship it became known as "The Castle." He sold in 1902 to Colton Russell, who converted it to a boarding house; it was purchased by Margaret Pattison in 1937, who removed the earthquake-damaged upper porch and tower.

Essence of Sunshine and Noir

Leonard Rose Mansion
400 South Grand Ave.
Curlett, Eisen & Cuthbertson
1887

Rose's residence was finished in exotic woods and parquetry floors. The stained glass windows were designed by Rose's son Guy, who became a celebrated Impressionist painter. Its ceiling frescoes were by Attilio Moretti. The third floor contained a ballroom.

George H. Stewart House
237 South Bunker Hill Ave.
George F. Costerisan (attr.) • ***1887***

▼ Stewart was a banker, councilman, and president of the Los Angeles Chamber of Commerce. Since he commissioned Costerisan to build a large addition to the back of the house in 1889, Costerisan is likely the architect of the original structure.

Lady McDonald Residence
321 South Bunker Hill Ave. • 1887/1891

▲ William Maynard's original house had the projecting "witch hat" corner bay; the north projection with the decorative truss was added by attorney George Ordway, who bought the house in 1891. It sold in 1892 to Frances Mitchell McDonald, also known as Lady McDonald, since she had been named a Canadian baroness.

Herman F. Baer House
221 South Olive St.
John Cotter Pelton • 1887

Baer sold to the Doran family in 1891, and it became a boarding house after its 1905 sale to investor R.A. Fowler. Its deep setback, ornate façade, and eventual lush overgrowth made it a photographer's favorite in its later days.

George Hugh Smith House
416 North Broadway • 1887

▶ The residence of G.H. Smith—lawyer, judge, state senator—was where the crème de la crème of the Old South held the town's most magnificent full-dress dances and cotillions. It became the home of Hancock Banning, who married Smith's daughter.

Milo S. Baker House
426 North Broadway
Samuel and Joseph Cather Newsom
1888

◄ The cellar of the Baker house was formed from the foundation of Fort Moore; builders had to remove pieces of cannon during excavation. The house had antique oak paneling, marquetry floors, a long parlor in pale gold with a frieze of palm leaves, and a winding stairway featuring nine different kinds of wood.

Judge Anson Brunson Mansion
350 South Grand Ave. • 1886/1888

Brunson's 1886 house was described as "an elegant, palatial residence." After the Rose mansion was built diagonally across the street in 1887, Brunson hired Abram Edelman to enlarge his house by raising it and adding a first story, at the then-enormous cost of $25,000.

Pierre Larronde House
237 North Hope St. • 1888

► William Byron Scarborough built this house in the spring of 1888, selling it in March 1889 to Pierre and Juana Larronde. Juana's daughters Mariana and Carolina Etchemendy still lived in the house in 1957, when it was taken over by eminent domain and demolished.

Bunker Hill, Los Angeles

Reverend Edward Hildreth Mansion
357 South Hope St.,
Joseph Cather Newsom • 1889

Built for a congregational minister from Chicago, this house shows Newsom in full Queen Anne mode, offering a dizzying array of surface treatments. The shingles swirl, the façade is pierced with multiple openings, balconies abound, and the chimney is a tour de force of bricklaying panache.

A series of tragedies befell the Hildreth family. Thereafter, the house had boarders until it was bought and restored by the Haufe family in 1946, although it was taken from them and demolished in the summer of 1953 to build a Harbor Freeway offramp.

Bunker Hill, Los Angeles

Almira Hershey Residence
350 South Grand Ave.
Oliver Perry Dennis (attr.) • 1896
Almira Hershey's house had a steeply pitched roof with candle-snuffer towers, made busier by its pinnacles and spires. Although its architect is unknown, she used Oliver Perry Dennis to design a similarly Châteauesque structure across the street in 1898.

Almira Hershey Residence Becomes the Castle Towers
750 West Fourth St.
Neher and Skilling • 1907
▶ Hershey moved her house to the bluff west of Hope Street, cut it in half and enlarged the structure, which would be known as the Castle Towers Apartments. It was demolished in 1954 for the Fourth Street Cut viaduct.

The Apartment Age

While less common than the large homes on Bunker Hill—a great number of which were cut up into apartments later in their lives—there was no lack of purpose-built apartment buildings constructed. There had been a number of gingerbread-trimmed duplexes before 1900 and a few Queen Anne-era apartment hotels, but the majority of apartment buildings were constructed after 1900. The Hill began to fall out of favor with homeowners as newer, more fashionable environs west of downtown were developed and the streetcar and automobile made access easier; meanwhile, the masses sought the experience of living on Bunker Hill. Building had slowed after the real estate bubble burst in 1887 and financial panics crashed the economy through the 1890s, but construction eventually reemerged with vigor, and with new styling: the Beaux-Arts. Popularized by the 1893 World's Columbian Exposition, Beaux-Arts style featured bilateral symmetry, the Classical orders, and Renaissance details like swags, garlands and cartouches. Tastemakers like Edward Bok and Edith Wharton stressed good proportion and simplicity as the expression of refinement. Mission Revival style also found favor after 1900. It was considerably less florid than the gingerbread of the 1880s; its clean lines and blank stucco walls prefigured Modernism.

Argyle
429 West Second St.
Robert Brown Young • 1887
The Argyle had one of the Hill's few examples of a mansard roof, which had fallen out of fashion by the mid-1880s. The Argyle lost its tower and the rest of its south façade to the Second Street Tunnel in 1921.

St. Angelo
237 North Grand Ave.
Curlett, Eisen & Cuthbertson • 1887
▶ The St. Angelo was a major Queen Anne apartment hotel, built at the height of the boom.

Melrose
130 South Grand Ave.
Joseph Cather Newsom • 1889
and Richelieu
142 South Grand Ave. • 1888

Retired oilman Marc William Connor built the Melrose both as his residence and boarding house; he lived there with his boarders until his death in 1912. Similarly, the home to the south had been built the year before by lumberman Robert Larkins, who kept boarders and called his establishment the Richelieu. Although its architect is unknown, its form suggests the hand of Bradbeer and Ferris.

Bunker Hill, Los Angeles

Melrose Annex
120 South Grand Ave.
Thomas J. McCarthy • 1902

The Melrose Annex is all bilateral symmetry, elaborated with festoons. Note the difference between it and Melrose (connected by skybridge) to its south. In 1908, architect George A. Howard extended the first floor to the sidewalk.

Colonial Flats
312–314 South Grand Ave.
Frederick Rice Dorn • 1902

▶ The Colonial Flats contained four apartments, finished in yellow pine. It was made all the more colonial with a "Captain's Walk" balustrade, as found on New England homes with views of the sea.

Earlcliff
231 South Bunker Hill Ave.
John Parkinson • 1903

Parkinson's design featured a giant order of engaged pilasters and a foliated frieze above the architrave, contrasting with the heavily Queen Anne style of the avenue.

Carleton
236 North Grand Ave.
Warren C. Dickerson • 1905

▼ Like the Colonial Flats, the Carleton featured a colossal order of Corinthian columns, but Dickerson looked to Greek Revival for inspiration, with a dentil-filled pediment applied to the elevation.

Nugent
257 South Grand Ave.
Robert E. Nelson • 1904

◀ Arthur Nugent McBurney's apartment house had a number of Beaux-Arts features like egg-and-dart molding, Corinthian capitals, and a cartouche within the pediment tympanum, although it also included a more Victorian corner tower. The Nugent was renamed the New Grand Hotel in 1940.

Majestic
700 West First St.
Millan Holmes • 1905
Lawrence Holmes built many apartments like this one that contain his Holmes Patented Disappearing Bed on rollers, which pulled out from the wall. The Majestic, designed by his brother Millan, was an incredible display of Corinthian capitals and heavily decorated cornices.

Essence of Sunshine and Noir

Marcella
223 South Flower St.
Garrett and Bixby • 1909

◀ Arthur and Bertha Fischer demolished their 1893 one-story frame dwelling in 1909, and built the fifty-four-room Marcella, which featured a giant order of fluted Corinthian columns and Tudor detailing on its bay windows.

Queen Apartments
529 California St.
John H. Brown • 1906

Emma Summers moved to Bunker Hill in 1887, taught piano, and from her modest means, began investing in oil wells. By 1900, her wells produced 50,000 barrels a month. Dubbed the Oil Queen of Los Angeles, Summers built the Queen Apartments, an amalgam of Beaux-Arts with wreaths, garlands, and Ionic capitals, but with pseudo-Moorish arches.

Fremont Hotel
401 South Olive St.
John C. Austin • 1902

◀ Named for explorer and politician John Charles Frémont, who as commander of the California Battalion had captured Los Angeles during the Mexican War, the Fremont was the first and largest of the Mission buildings on the Hill, and featured the red tile, towers, and parapets that defined the style. The hotel's first guest was its namesake's widow, Jessie Benton Frémont.

Mission Apartments
201 South Olive St.
Arthur L. Haley • 1905

This apartment house had various early names (including "The Schloesser," after the folks who took up the lease in 1906), but gained its best-known and most appropriate moniker, the Mission Apartments, in 1910.

Ems
321 South Olive St.
Joseph Cather Newsom • 1905

▼ J.C. Newsom relocated to San Francisco in 1890 but returned to Los Angeles in 1905; one of his first commissions was an apartment hotel for Charles Clayton Emswiler. The eponymous Ems was erected in full Mission vernacular, including verandas, many rounded arches, twin red-tile towers, and a large decorative chimney.

Bunker Hill, Los Angeles

Minnewaska/Dome
201 South Grand Ave.
James M. Shields • 1903

The Minnewaska (renamed the Dome in 1929) has a curious design, born of the Mission vernacular. With its cream-colored plaster, red tile, and curving parapets, the apartment building features a dome more evocative of Eastern European or Indo-Islamic architecture.

Granada
419 South Grand Ave.
Charles O. Ellis • 1903

▼ Architect Ellis designed a cement-on-lath exterior with Mission parapets and a sixty-foot arcade. The design includes a crenellated parapet—unusual for Mission Revival; Ellis also crenellated the roofline of the Beaux-Arts style Lovejoy apartments one block north.

Life on the Hill

Many people considered Bunker Hill a slum, justly suited for demolition, infected as it was with cinematic rot and decrepitude. True, its residents were poor. When Los Angeles Housing Authority photographer Leonard Nadel captured the typical resident as an alcoholic pack rat, that might have been a fair depiction. The *Los Angeles Times* labeled Bunker Hill a "crime haunt," but the term looks hollow when historians investigate the area, reviewing photographs and interviewing former residents. The area was a functioning neighborhood; there were churches, schools, theaters, clubhouse buildings, and plenty of local places to shop. In the postwar era, this sort of pedestrian-friendly environment was anathema to the prevailing cultural sentiment, in which a brave new modernity favored a suburban shopping center serviced by an acre of parking lot. Rather, people on Bunker Hill walked and talked. They might head to Pershing Square for the day to watch public speakers pontificate or simply lounge on the benches where Third Street ended at Bunker Hill Avenue. Those who lived on the Hill in the 1950s recall the sound of cooing pigeons, opera emanating from a window over the dim rush of the city below, or the smell of frying steaks competing with the scent of a profusion of flowers. Like its people, its pace was slow and quiet—anachronistic in the Jet Age.

Bunker Hill, Los Angeles

The Benches
Third Street and Bunker Hill Avenue
"They sat there on the bench at the top of Bunker Hill, looking down at the cars sailing along the Harbor Freeway, listening to the wind rattling the stiff palm fronds. ... It was pleasant in the quiet spot above the city's noise. The sun felt good after a week of clouds and smog. The old man turned to another elderly man sitting beside him. 'I've lived up here 45 years,' he said. 'Nothing new has been built up here in all that time. And look what's been going on all around us.'"
—*Los Angeles Times*, January 29, 1956

Life at the Norfolk Apartments
820 West First St.
▲ Inside the Norfolk Apartments (Train & Williams, 1909). This image was shot by Leonard Nadel for the Community Redevelopment Agency (CRA). Nadel added notes about the occupants and standards, like "illegal kitchen" or "hazardous wiring." On this negative, he scribbled "820 W 1st. Unit 36. Slum. $42/mo—2 rooms. 'pack rat.' 9/30/55."

Life at 209 South Bunker Hill Ave.
From a Nadel group marked Substandard Housing. Written on the negative's glassine envelope: "Rent $25/mo. Outside toilet. 81 yrs. old—14 yrs. residence. 10/5/55." The building at 209 was home to several early gentrifiers, including *Los Angeles Times* columnist Joan Winchell. Winter Horton, broadcasting pioneer and cofounder of KCET-TV, lived next door at 203. Winchell, comparing Los Angeles to San Francisco, described Bunker Hill as "the south's answer to Telegraph Hill," the City by the Bay's bohemian enclave. 1955.

The Hildreth Becomes Hopecrest
357 South Hope St.
▶ Contrary to the prevailing narrative that the Hill was in irrevocable decline, Angelenos moved there to renovate. John and Mabel Haufe purchased the Hildreth in 1946 and began restoration, renaming it Hopecrest. 1950.

Bunker Hill, Los Angeles

A Child in Squalor

▶ All the purported elements of Bunker Hill: ramshackle tenements—in this case, the backside of the Bishop Apartments at 334 South Figueroa St.—battered bins full of trash, a blackened incinerator, and a boy who looks as sad as his surroundings. 1955.

Children at Play

At the same time, children were healthy and happy at the Bunker Hill Playground and Recreation Center, a half-acre exercise and amusement area, including a recreation hall complete with stage, classrooms, kitchen, and showers. 1955.

Essence of Sunshine and Noir

Third Street and Grand Avenue
Third Street, west of Olive Street, was once the main commercial zone of Bunker Hill. It embodied the axioms of today's urban planners, whose mixed-use developments emphasize walkability, human scale, and neighborhood character. Says the pharmacist in the documentary short *Bunker Hill 1956*: "… it solves the problem of the big city, you could live there for two hundred years and you're still nobody. But up on Bunker Hill, people are somebody … it's kind of a small town atmosphere." February 1963.

Bernhard Sens/Dr. James Green House
232 South Grand Ave. • *1894*

◀ Originally the home of bespoke tailor Bernhard Sens, Dr. James Green moved in in 1929 and became primary physician for the Hill's residents until his death in 1956. Green accepted very little in payment, and is said to have delivered thousands of babies during his long practice.

Bunker Hill, Los Angeles

Lux Theater
827 West Third St.
Train & Williams • 1914

▲ The 500-seat Lux opened as the Bear Theatre in 1914. It wasn't just a movie theater; evangelists preached on stage during the Depression. Other theaters on the Hill included the short-lived Tunnel Theatre one block east, and the Hunt and Burns-designed College Theatre on Hill Street.

Congregation Beth Israel
227 North Olive St.
Smith & Elder • 1902

Congregation Beth Israel was formed in 1899 with the merging of three orthodox congregations. Their temple was Moorish Revival—the popular synagogue style of the time, intended to connote the Golden Age of Jewish culture during the time of Al-Andalus.

Sons of the Revolution Headquarters and Library
437 South Hope St.
Dodd & Richards • 1928

▶ Sons of the Revolution are a genealogical organization whose members trace their lineage back to the Revolutionary War. Dodd and Richards added a bit of Americanism to their headquarters' design by evoking Philadelphia's Independence Hall in the fenestration.

B.P.O.E. Temple, Lodge No. 99
300 South Olive St.
Hudson and Munsell • 1909

The Benevolent and Protective Order of the Elks dedicated its new temple, on the site of the old Crocker mansion, in May 1909. It was an imposing presence with quoins, projecting cornice, and stained glass. The Olive Street front was the annex, housing dormitories; its lodge rooms were in a back building over Clay Street.

Bunker Hill, Los Angeles

Olive Street School
419 South Olive St.
Charles Lincoln Strange • 1896
▲ Olive Street School educated preteen children until its 1909 conversion into a high school and evening school. It was a Board of Education administration building when damaged by fire in October 1922, and demolished in early 1923.

Nearing the End
In this image, author/photographer Arnold Hylen strolls along upper Hope Street, in a self-portrait from 1962, with 632 West Third St. beside him. Of the Hill's final moments, Hylen wrote: "The last days were filled with rancor and bitterness. The beleaguered residents, realizing the futility of their resistance, frequently took a hostile attitude toward the world in general. Who could blame them? There was no longer any room for their little haven in a world of monoliths."

Essence of Sunshine and Noir

Homes of Notable Folk

Among Bunker Hill's populace lived some of Los Angeles's most influential and unorthodox folk: famed architects Greene and Greene stayed in the Nugent at 257 South Grand Ave.; young Edith Claire Posener—before she became designer Edith Head—while enrolled at Los Angeles High School up on Fort Moore, arranged a dance for her class in the grand ballroom on the fourth floor of her apartment-house, the Zelda, at 401 South Grand Ave.; a young Marion Morrison lived at the Gladden, 100 South Olive St., before he became John Wayne; and Lon Cheney Sr. bunked at the Storer Apartments, at 123 N. Grand Ave. Here are the homes of some other folk who seem endemic to Bunker Hill, defining its particular if not somewhat oddball nature.

Margrethe Mather
715 West Fourth St.

Margrethe Mather was, between 1915 and 1935, one of America's best-known female photographers. She kept her studio in the carriage house behind the Hildreth mansion.

Jack Webb
237 South Flower St.

◀ Actor and producer Jack Webb grew up with his mother and grandmother in the St. Regis apartments between 1921 and 1938. Perhaps Bunker Hill's decrepitude motivated him to picture a greater, better-functioning hometown when he created the hit radio and television crime drama *Dragnet*.

Divine Order of the Royal Arms of the Great Eleven
355 South Grand Ave.
▶ In 1922, May Otis Blackburn claimed she and her daughter were charged by archangels to reveal the secrets of heaven and earth; their subsequent fraud trial revealed sex scandals, murder, and the attempt to resurrect a sixteen-year-old-girl through mummification and animal sacrifice.

Max Heindel and Augusta Foss
315 South Bunker Hill Ave.
▼ In 1909, young mystic Max Heindel met Augusta Foss in his boarding house (in the home her family had built circa 1885). Discovering they shared a penchant for esoteric theology, Heindel and Foss formulated the Rosicrucian Fellowship, a melding of the Bible and spiritual astrology.

Don Slater and Antonio Reyes
221 South Bunker Hill Ave.
▶ The home of "Dauntless" Don Slater and Tony Reyes was where the articles of incorporation for One, Inc., the first gay rights organization in the United States, were drafted in November 1952.

Essence of Sunshine and Noir

The Hill in Art

Bunker Hill was often depicted in fine art. Its fading mansions allured painters, amateur and professional, who wished to capture the wistful, disappearing world. Trained artists such as Emil Kosa Jr. and Ben Abril produced Hill-themed canvases. Marcel Cavalla, though, simply sat on his porch painting the houses in his simple, geometric style when "discovered" by Jerry Jerome of the Ceeje Galleries.

Millard Sheets, Angel's Flight • 1931

▼ Millard Sheets was a titan of California Scene Painting; *Angel's Flight* is generally acknowledged as his masterpiece. The titular flight is not shown, though the surrounding structures are identifiable, including the Hillcrest and Sunshine Apartments. The buildings are disjointed, and the steps snake their way up from—and down into—the darkness.

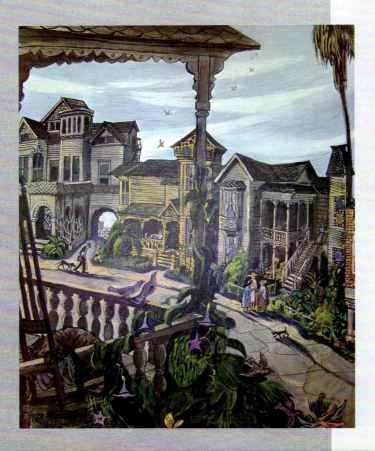

Leo Politi, South Bunker Hill Avenue • Circa 1958

◀ Author and artist Leo Politi's book *Bunker Hill Los Angeles: Reminiscences of Bygone Days*, contains gouache and watercolor images of the Hill. Politi said he aimed to capture a house's soul; he also spoke to tenants to gain insight into each home's history. He is renowned for twenty-plus children's books illustrated with his paintings, focusing on Olvera Street.

The Work of Kay Martin

▶ Catherine "Kay" Martin was known and lauded during the 1950s for her work depicting the Hill, with solo shows and awards in statewide competitions. Martin wanted her paintings to hang on Bunker Hill, and they did, finally, in the Angelus Plaza retirement complex, until 2014. When the CRA disbanded, her records were discarded and paintings put in storage.

Bunker Hill Noir

Old Bunker Hill will likely always be associated with crime and decrepitude, filled with grifters and ruffians, a haunt of the dissolute and debauched. "Juvenile, as well as adult, crime flourishes in the transient, unsavory atmosphere of Bunker Hill" read a 1956 police report. Low rents after World War I had made the Hill attractive to transients, mostly older men of spotty employment. Admittedly, Bunker Hill did have higher-than-average rates of crime, incidences of narcotic abuse, and juvenile delinquency, but a 1947 City Planning Commission study found that when it came to blight, contributing influences including juvenile delinquency, low rents, and substandard dwellings, Bunker Hill fared better than large swaths of Los Angeles. Nevertheless, the Hill certainly had its share of problem areas; one police report identified Clay Street, the areas around Second and Figueroa Streets and Third and Flower Streets as the primary zones of narcotics abuse. The two blocks of Third Street between Hope and Figueroa Streets were thick with bars—in the late-1950s these included the Pitch Inn, the Paradise Inn, Sam's Bowery, Jack's Café, Lou's Café, Bob's Café, the Best Café, the Porthole, Club 801, and the Fig Leaf. Part of Bunker Hill's enduring fascination is its reputation for crime propagated by cinema: films such as *The Killing*, *Kiss Me Deadly*, *Act of Violence*, etc. In this section we take a look at a smattering of real-world crimes from the Hill's history.

A Crime of Passion at the Boswell
245 South Flower St.   February 26, 1925
Timothy Yatko surprised his wife Lola and her paramour Harry Kidder, in their Boswell lovenest, fatally stabbing Kidder in the throat. At the trial, where normally a wife would not be allowed to testify against her husband, the judge ruled their wedding illegal, as California Civil Code prohibited interracial marriage (Yatko was Filipino).

Bunker Hill, Los Angeles

Alta Vista
255 South Bunker Hill Ave.
James M. Shields • 1902

◀ The Alta Vista opened in the fall of 1902, four stories in front, seven stories running down to Hope Street in back. It saw fires, murders, and the filming of many noir movies before being demolished for safety violations in 1957. Robert and Harriett Allen were shacked up in their honeymoon apartment, room 406, married just eight days. Harriet had once been Bruce Moore's sweetheart. There was an early morning knock on their door on August 12, 1933. "Bob, hurry up, Bruce is here!" were Harriett's final words; Bruce fired five shots into her as she ran into the bedroom, turning the final bullet on himself. Bob was left shaken, dazed, and alone.

Astoria Apartments
248 South Olive St.
Arthur L. Haley • 1905

▼ The Astoria, with its deep arcaded porch and red-tile tower, was one of Haley's several Mission Revival structures on the Hill. It would be visited by the Brickbat Killer April 4, 1937. Robert Nixon perpetrated a dozen rapes, beatings, and murders in Los Angeles. Nixon's usual tool, a brick, earned him the sobriquet "The Brickbat Killer." Nixon and accomplice Howard Green broke into Room 206 of the Astoria where they assaulted and murdered Edna Worden and her twelve-year-old daughter Marguerite. Fingerprints left at the Astoria led to Nixon's 1939 conviction and execution.

Essence of Sunshine and Noir

An Obscene Proposal at the Lovejoy
529 West Third St. — November 5, 1947

Charles Vuykov, 52, was found nude and killed by a .25 slug, in his apartment at the Lovejoy. Vuykov's murder would have likely gone unsolved had Gerald Lee Richards, 19, not shot at the Biltmore manager with his .25 the next day. Richards confessed to Vuykov's murder, the result, he asserted, of "obscene proposals" to the young sailor. Richards got ten to life at San Quentin and was paroled in April 1958; he went on a holdup spree, and died in a gun battle with Houston police that September.

Cops Are Here Again
Circa 1962
The law has come to wheel someone out of Bob's Café, 708 West Third St. This cocktail joint was one of many west of the Third Street Tunnel.

Essence of Sunshine and Noir

Hill Street

Hill Street, north of Fifth Street, was once a grand commercial thoroughfare, with both the east and west sides lined with height-limit steel-reinforced office buildings, two- and three-story brick hotels, movie theaters, and other commercial ventures. Hill Street was originally residential, populated with cottages and apartment buildings in the days before homes crept up the Hill. Over the years the ornate Victorian homes and apartment houses fell and were replaced by a work, shopping and entertainment destination for Bunker Hill residents. Angels Flight was added to Hill Street in 1901, helping Bunker Hill residents make their way up the Hill and down to the city with greater ease. With the Depression and after World War Two, as downtown declined, Hill Street took on an air of dissolution. Pool halls, pawn shops, watering holes, and other low-rent establishments proliferated. One by one, the buildings were demolished and the streetscape erased in the years between 1965 and 1970. Clay Street, which ran parallel to Hill Street between Second and Fourth Streets, was returned to its early, earthy roots; one could again see the clay deposits on the cliffs that had given the street its name. Hill Street saw the demolition of its twin bore tunnels north of First Street (and the hill that contained them) in 1955 and the removal of its beloved Angels Flight in 1969. Hill Street was slowly, mostly, redeveloped, including the return of Angels Flight in 1996.

Hill Street North from Second Street
April 1906
Left to Right: Locke House, built by Mrs. Julia E. Locke in 1894, demolished 1918; Albert Stephens house, circa 1883, demolished 1912; the Moore Cliff (Dennis and Farwell, 1905); Howard M. Sale house, 1889, converted to the Hotel El Moro in 1901.

Hotel Lincoln
211 South Hill St.
Costerisan and Forsyth • 1888

▲ The Lincoln was one the grandest of the Queen Anne hotels, known for its large and elegant dining room—"the cuisine defies competition," wrote the *Evening Express* in June 1888.

Hill Street between Third and Second Streets
Circa 1888

The residential character of Hill Street after the boom. At far left is 257 South Hill St., the home of Rose McCoy, a house that would be moved up Third and replaced by the McCoy Block in 1905.

Masonic Temple
431 South Hill St.
Bradbeer and Ferris • 1896

▶ This massive Masonic temple held multiple lodges, and kept a Scottish Rite cathedral on the third floor. It was finished in salmon-colored pressed brick, Sespe sandstone, and terra cotta. Pacific Electric purchased it in 1915, and remodeled it for use by its 4200 employees.

Third and Hill Streets • September 1910
◀ Hill Street grew quickly after the turn of the century. Along with Angels Flight came the George Wyman-designed Hulburt apartments and Ferguson office building, seen here under construction. The McCoy Block, right (Morgan and Walls, 1905), was built as a Seventh-day Adventist sanitorium, offering vegetarian meals and colonics.

University Club
349 South Hill St.
John Parkinson • 1904
▶ The University Club built its South Hill Street space in the summer of 1904 and remained until 1921. The Hill Street building was later remodeled into the lodge rooms for the Native Sons of the Golden West.

The Vegetarian Café
259 South Hill St.
▲ To the initiated, vegetarianism was more than a change of eating habits; it would affect social reform. Reformers argued that meat-eating caused crime and that abstaining would cure drunkenness. The café remained at the location through 1920.

Cowper Homestead Property
Northwest Corner Fourth and Hill Streets
▶ A collection of frame dwellings, the last of old Hill Street, before being replaced by the Black Building. Across Clay Street, Hotel Antlers (Robert Brown Young, 1902), and at right, the Roberts Block (Robert Brown Young, 1904). 1911.

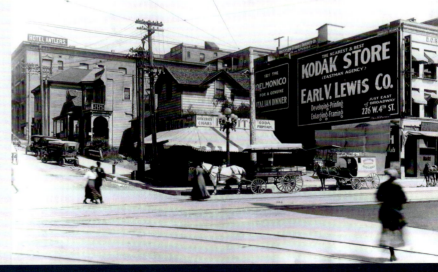

Essence of Sunshine and Noir

Hill Street
The two-story house with the pyramidal hipped roof, left, stood at 331/329 South Hill St., and the striped-roof Ferguson house (John Hall, 1886) is on the corner at Third Street. Circa 1890.

Changes on Hill Street
▶ A three-story loft and commercial structure (Albert C. Martin, 1913) now stands at 331/329 South Hill St. The Ferguson Building, with the large projecting cornice, stands on the corner, replacing the Ferguson house. 1938

Bunker Hill, Los Angeles

Essence of Sunshine and Noir

Wright and Callender Building
403 South Hill St.
Austin and Brown • 1908

◀ This steel-framed Beaux-Arts office building was noted for its large marble and tile lobby, and use of marble throughout its halls. Architects John C. Austin, Elmer Grey, and the team of Meyer and Holler kept offices in the building.

Black Building
361 South Hill St.
Edelman and Barnett • 1913

▶ The gleaming white Black Building was a glazed terra cotta Beaux-Arts height-limit office structure, with an interior paneled in mahogany, marble, and tile.

YWCA
251 South Hill St.
Arthur Burnett Benton • 1908

▶▶ The Young Women's Christian Association built its headquarters with a 500-seat auditorium, swimming pool, and enormous light well with cascading flower boxes. It became the main office for the Union League in 1919, and it was converted to the Hotel Belmont in 1924.

The passage in stained glass in the lobby is John 10:10, "I am come that they might have life, and that they might have it more abundantly." This was removed when converted to the Hotel Belmont.

Essence of Sunshine and Noir

In the Pool Parlor
▲ Inside the pool hall on the ground floor of the Pembroke Hotel, 339 South Hill St. Circa 1959.

300 Block of Hill Street
▶ Downtown declined during the Depression and the postwar years; freeways, suburbanization, and shopping malls led to the abandonment of the central business district.

    R to L: Doran Building (Austin and Brown, 1904); Pembroke Hotel (Austin and Brown, 1905); Wright and Callender Block (Parkinson and Bergstrom, 1905); University Club (John Parkinson, 1904); Roberts Block (Robert Brown Young, 1904); Black Building (Edelman and Barnett, 1913). 1962.

Cinderella's for Hot Dogs
▲ A man grabs a bite and a moment's flapjaw, just south of the Third Street Tunnel, at the base of the Luckenbach Building. This was a handy place to pick up a pack of smokes and get a shoeshine. Circa 1960.

Bunker Hill, Los Angeles

Essence of Sunshine and Noir

Fort Moore Hill

The boundaries of Bunker Hill are normally accepted as running from Fifth Street north to Sunset Boulevard. It was once covered with an unbroken swath of homes and apartments, sharing the same scenic overlook, constructed in the same era, and having met the same fate. The northern quarter of the Bunker Hill area, north of Temple Street, is usually known as Fort Moore Hill, after the military breastwork built there in the 1840s; but its association with Bunker Hill endures. For example when the 1887 Giese house at 840 West Sunset—on the far northern end of Fort Moore—was illegally demolished in 2003, the papers declared "Last House in Bunker Hill Razed." Though Fort Moore Hill has a thematic and geographical twinship with Bunker Hill, Fort Moore Hill does have its own unique identity. It was the site of two Los Angeles high schools. It harbored the first Protestant cemetery in Los Angeles. It was also the scene of bizarre explorations involving x-rays, gold tablets and lizard-men. Like Bunker Hill, little of it is left, most taken by the Hollywood freeway, much in the way that a good chunk of Bunker Hill was taken by the Harbor Freeway's Fourth Street offramp.

Hill Cemetery
A Protestant cemetery was formally dedicated in 1862, but after the City took over control, schools were built atop its grounds (note the towers of the 1890 high school). Students vandalized the cemetery. Countless bodies were disinterred when the freeway cut through, and when the new high school was built in 2004. 1906.

Bunker Hill, Los Angeles

Fort Moore Hill
At right, the Col. Smith/Hancock Banning house; at center is the Harry Chandler house. One block west is Hill Street, where red-brick Los Angeles High School was built on cemetery property in 1890; the dense wooded area, behind, is more abandoned cemetery. 1899.

Fort Moore Hill, After the Tunnel
▶ The Broadway Tunnel opened in August 1901. Forty feet wide and 750 feet long, it stretched to Sunset Boulevard. It was demolished in 1949 for the Hollywood Freeway.

Essence of Sunshine and Noir

Los Angeles Public High School
Ezra Kysor • 1872
▲ The Italianate structure, built on Poundcake Hill to the east, was hoisted onto Fort Moore in 1886. After a long fight by alumni to save the school, it was demolished in 1949.

Harry Chandler House
503 North Broadway • 1894
◀ Harry Chandler married the boss's daughter in 1894; his father-in-law, *Los Angeles Times* publisher Harrison Gray Otis, bought this house for the newlyweds. From their perch, Harry and son Norman watched the 1912 construction of the 150-foot clock tower of the third building to house the *Times*.

The Lost Empire of Lizard Men
◀ In the early 1930s, geophysical engineer George Warren Shufelt, searching for buried doubloons beneath Fort Moore via his "radio X-ray device," was soon chasing after a mythical empire of the Lizard People, whose supposed five-thousand-year-old tunnels were filled with enormous gold tablets, inscribed with the origins of the human race. January 1934.

Bunker Hill, Los Angeles

On Fort Moore Hill
Looking across the wide south lawn of the Wills's house, across Fort Moore Place to the Baker house on the corner of Broadway.

Essence of Sunshine and Noir

Motive Power

Los Angeles is permanently associated with automobiles, since the town grew into a sprawling metropolis alongside the car, as both rose in cultural importance. The metro area is defined by freeways, drive-ins, and mimetic architecture designed to attract passing motorists. Bunker Hill's relationship with transport is deep and particular. Robert M. Widney, who lived on Hill Street at the base of Bunker Hill, pioneered mass transit: when he tired of trekking from Hill Street into the business section of town every day, he developed a horse-drawn single-track railroad that passed by his house. Early cable cars passed up and down Bunker Hill, and two funiculars, Angels Flight and Court Flight, helped residents ascend the heights.

Bunker Hill's residents had famously few cars, but downtown parking lot developers eyed the Hill as an opportunity, buying homes to demolish and build garages; Los Angeles's first parking lot was developed by Andrew Pansini at Fourth and Olive in 1917.

Where transit wasn't going up the Hill, it went through. The Hill had long been seen as a barrier to the natural westward expansion of Los Angeles, and having to pass over it was difficult. Boring through the Hill was the logical choice, with tunnels piercing east-west via Second and Third Streets, and north-south via Hill Street and Broadway; Hill and Fourth Streets was also the location of Los Angeles's subway, where the Pacific Electric ran underground beneath Bunker Hill.

Bunker Hill, Los Angeles

Hill Street Tunnel Demolition • May 1955
◀ The Hill Street tunnels, and the hill above, were demolished as part of the Civic Center County Courthouse/Hall of Administration project. Bulldozers and steam shovels tore the hill apart, and dynamite blasted the remains.

Hill Street Tunnels
▲ In 1903, Hill Street business owners began pressing the Board of Public Works to bore a tunnel under Hill Street between First and Temple, to ease bottlenecks. The Board of Public Works-designed tunnel wasn't built, but it did inspire Los Angeles–Pacific Railway to bore a tunnel for interurban rail cars in 1909. The City added a second tunnel for automobiles in 1913. 1919.

Essence of Sunshine and Noir

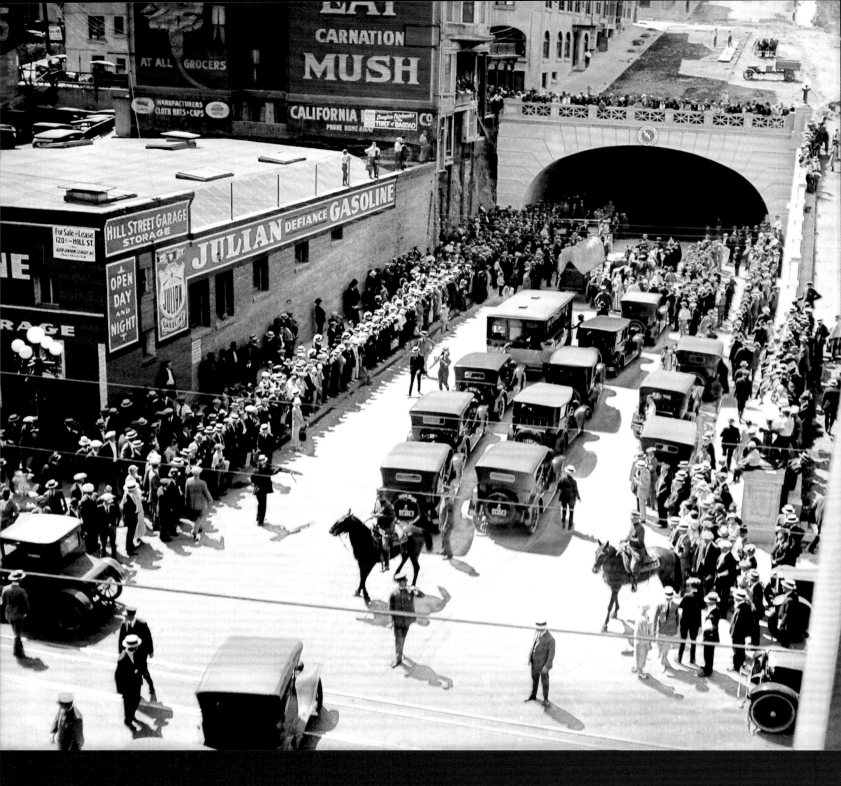

Bunker Hill, Los Angeles

Pacific Electric Train Depot
421 South Hill St.
John Parkinson • 1916

▲ Pacific Electric's Bunker Hill station, with a Parkinson-designed train depot and, at left, a Mission Revival station house (Hunt, Eager and Burns, 1908), was demolished in early 1925 for a subway terminal.

Pacific Electric Subway Terminal Building
417 South Hill St.
Schultze and Weaver • 1925

▶ Pacific Electric built a 600-office, granite- and terra cotta Renaissance Revival terminal building for its underground railway. It ran a mile northwest, to the intersection of Beverly and Glendale Boulevards, carrying an average of 50,000 people daily.

Second Street Tunnel • 1924

◀ Despite construction of the Third Street, Hill Street, and Broadway tunnels, the Second Street Tunnel was approved in 1916 to alleviate downtown congestion. It formally opened July 25, 1924 with Cheyenne Chief White Antelope leading Acting Mayor Boyle Workman through the tunnel in a covered wagon.

Essence of Sunshine and Noir

The Hotel Clark Garage
350 South Olive St.
Dodd & Richards • 1919
As automobile usage increased, it became necessary to park and service cars near the central business district. The Hill's southern slope was soon eyed as a suitable site for garages. The first was the Hotel Clark Garage (renamed Center Garage in 1950). The elephants seen here were paraded through the streets in May 1953 on their way to shoot the movie *Elephant Walk*. 1953.

Bunker Hill, Los Angeles

**The Savoy Auto Park
400 South Olive St.
Curlett & Beelman • 1923**

▲ The Savoy Auto Park at Fourth and Olive necessitated demolition of William and Robert Widney's old homes. The Savoy is the oldest extant parking garage in Los Angeles.

**Grand Central Garage
535 West Fifth St.
Forest Q. Stanton • 1920**

The Grand Central Garage "motor car hotel" contained nine acres of floor space (largest garage in the world) with stalls for 1,100 automobiles, gas and oil on each level, and an auto repair shop.

Essence of Sunshine and Noir

The Modern Age

For those with only a passing knowledge of Bunker Hill, it is commonly believed that all buildings were Victorian (just as many believe that all its residents were characters from a Raymond Chandler novel). Yet, while the Hill certainly had a high percentage of structures built before 1900, studying only its early architecture fails to tell the whole story. The Hill shall never be famous for its Modern structures, but there were some remarkable buildings, now lost, that deserve attention.

The length of Fifth Street was especially notable for its collection of art deco monuments, two of which remain today, the Edison and Title Guarantee buildings. On the Hill proper were significant updates to the built landscape: modern gas stations, neon signage, glass brick. In defiance of the popular conception of Bunker Hill as simply a tangled, overgrown nest of decay, there was even Space Age Googie detailing.

These lost examples of Modernism serve to remind us of overlooked and underrecognized Bunker Hill—it was not just a place frozen in time, but an ever-evolving neighborhood.

People's National Bank
439 South Hill St.
Walker and Eisen • 1928

People's National (also known as National Bank of Commerce, and Federal Title) was noted for its elaborate figural friezes by Salvatore Cartaino Scarpitta. The building remained completely unaltered throughout its life, until demolition in 1985.

Bunker Hill, Los Angeles

Title Guarantee and Trust Company
411 West Fifth St.
John Parkinson • 1930

Parkinson designed Title Guarantee, according to the *Los Angeles Times*, in a "modernized vertical Gothic of restrained ornament," being shorthand for an art deco office building with a flying buttress-adorned setback tower. Its sculpted reliefs are by Eugene Maier-Krieg, and the interior murals are by Hugo Ballin.

State Mutual Building and Loan Association
415 West Fifth St.
William Richards • 1931

▼ State Mutual's stone-and-aluminum façade by William Richards featured stylized bas-relief of builders holding plans for State Mutual structures, executed by Salvatore Cartaino Scarpitta.

Temple Baptist Auditorium
435 West Fifth St.
Charles F. Whittlesey • 1906

▲▲ Whittlesey was known for his work in concrete, and when built this was the largest concrete building in the world, with the largest cantilevered balcony. Temple Auditorium was utilized as a church, movie theater, and was the home of the Los Angeles Philharmonic after 1920.

Temple Auditorium Remodel
Claud Beelman • Fall 1938

▲ By the 1930s, the picturesque excesses of the auditorium were seen as hopelessly antiquated. The Auditorium Company hired Claud Beelman to remove its mansard roof and streamline the exterior in a massive façade remodel.

The Auditorium Hotel
511 West Fifth St.
Neher and Skilling • 1910

▲▲ The Auditorium Hotel, built across the street from Temple Auditorium, was designed to complement the church and its lavish ornamentation. Like Temple Auditorium, it was eventually deemed too ornate.

The Auditorium Hotel Gets a Streamlining

▲ Renamed the San Carlos in 1930, much of its ornamentation was stripped between 1939 and 1940, with cornices removed in 1946. The jaunty Armét and Davis-designed Googies and San Carlos Room date to 1956.

The Southern California Edison Building
601 West Fifth St. Allison and Allison • 1931
One of the first all-electrically heated and cooled setback-style office towers. Its entrance loggia features Robert Merrell Gage's allegorical bas-relief sculptures of light, power, and hydroelectric energy; its lobby contains murals by Hugo Ballin, Conrad Buff, and Barse Miller.

Sunkist Building for the California Fruit Growers Exchange
707 West Fifth St.
Walker and Eisen • 1935

▲ The Sunkist Building was a monumental art deco expression in cast concrete. Its façade featured concrete bas-relief panels by Harold F. Wilson, with interior murals by Frank Bowers and Arthur Prunier. 1954.

Monarch Hotel
905 West Fifth St.
Cramer and Wise • 1929

The Monarch Hotel was known for its blazing red neon sign above the penthouse, private roof decks, and art deco furniture from Barker Brothers.

Federation of Jewish Welfare Organizations
610 West Temple St.
Marcus P. Miller • 1933

▼ 610 West Temple, built as a lodging house in 1915, received an art deco remodel by architect Marcus Phillips Miller.

Bunker Hill, Los Angeles

Avalon Apartments
144 South Grand Ave. • *1940*
The 1883 house of pioneering water pipe manufacturer Nathan Wilson Stowell was demolished in 1938 by building-owner Henry E. Rivers, who built this Streamline four-unit apartment building dubbed the Avalon. April 1957.

Essence of Sunshine and Noir

Angels Flight Café
501 West Third St.
The shops (Alfred Franklin Priest, 1911) at the northwest corner of Third and Olive Streets, became the Angels Flight Café in 1933, and were given a glass brick-and-aluminum Streamline remodel in December 1936 by Weber Showcase and Fixture Company. December 1962.

Pacific Telephone Complex
420–434 South Grand Ave.
Charles Day Woodford • 1947
Woodford and Bernard • 1962/1966
Southern California Telephone began purchasing and demolishing structures on Grand Avenue behind its headquarters at 433 South Olive St. in 1945, and began construction of a connecting Late Moderne building. In 1962, Pacific Telephone added a third building noted for its 185-foot, 250-ton radio microwave antenna support. This tower was demolished in 1966; eight stories were added to the base structure, and then rebuilt in an updated configuration. June 1962.

Essence of Sunshine and Noir

Early Demolition

Bunker Hill was famously reduced to rubble by the bulldozers of the 1960s redevelopment movement, the product of a government plan that promoted slum clearance for urban renewal. Bunker Hill, though, had been the target of renovation schemes throughout the preceding decades. The Hill was seen as a barrier to progress: to the growth of the downtown business district, to the development of the Civic Center, to the free flow of traffic.

While none of the grand redevelopment plans proffered came to pass, several large-scale projects cut into the Hill. Though the Community Redevelopment Agency (CRA) managed to purchase most of the area between Fifth and First Streets after 1960, it is important to remember that the Hill as it stretched northward from First was removed by the County for Civic Center expansion, and north of Temple in the Fort Moore area was demolished for a freeway and school buildings. Many landmarks were felled at the hands of their owners, to become apartment buildings, garages, or parking lots.

Demolition of the Bradbury Mansion • February 1929

The Bradbury mansion, which had cost $80,000 to build in 1886, was sold for $250. As it was dismantled for a parking lot, scores of folk ascended the Hill to walk the polished marble steps one final time, and recount memories of dancing in the mansion in the Gay '90s.

Bunker Hill, Los Angeles

Fourth Street Cut
Hugo H. Winter/Lloyd Aldrich • 1954
▲ The Fourth Street Cut, a major offramp from the Harbor Freeway across Bunker Hill into downtown, opened May 1, 1956. The image illustrates the path it took and some of the twenty-three buildings demolished; the steps at bottom-center once led to the doors of the Fremont Hotel.

The Richelieu's End • 1957
▶ The Richelieu, as built in 1888 by Robert Larkins — the carved center panel contains an "RL" — remained remarkably intact to the end.

    The Department of Building and Safety permit from April 24, 1957, simply shows the Richelieu's owner to be the County of Los Angeles and the contractor to be National House Wrecking and Salvage, with a property valuation of $950.

Essence of Sunshine and Noir

*The Demolition of the Melrose
June 1957*
▲ The County took the three-block area bounded by First, Hill, Second, and Hope Streets in 1957, clearing sixty-plus structures, including the Melrose. No new permanent structures were built on these properties until 2003.

Inside the Melrose
Urban explorer Virgil Mirano shot this image inside the Melrose before its demolition. It shows its Lincrusta, a deeply embossed wall covering made of linseed oil and pressed wood pulp. May 1957.

*Sherwood Apartments
431 South Grand Ave.
Meyer and Holler • 1913*
▶ The Sherwood had a fountain in an inglenook on its full-width porch, a large fireplace in its mahogany-paneled lobby, and its rooms and hallways were much more capacious than required by law.

▶▶ The Sherwood was purchased by Southern California Edison, which demolished it for employee parking in September 1957. The CRA took over the lot in 1984, and the area became the site of a new street named Hope Place.

Bunker Hill, Los Angeles

The CRA Years

When Los Angeles City Council greenlit the Bunker Hill Urban Renewal Project in 1959, and the Community Redevelopment Agency began purchasing homes and undertaking demolitions in 1961, the Hill became a very different place for residents. Homes and businesses were boarded up. The Hill's nearly ten thousand residents, ensconced in their homes, became accustomed to the daily roar of bulldozers and the crunch of timber. One by one, their neighborhood shops went out of business, until once-familiar landmarks simply vanished. Finally, the people themselves were shuttled through the rooms of the CRA relocation offices, converted from the old Victorian home at 232 South Grand Ave. "Some [residents] had their roots in old Bunker Hill as deep as those of an oak," said the *Los Angeles Times* in February 1962. "And transplanting oneself in the winter of life, away from friends, away from each ancient landmark, is like uprooting the old oak itself." The "ancient landmarks" were but fifty to seventy-five years old. Some residents hung on as long as they could, watching as gleaming new Modernist structures rose across First Street, an augur of the Hill's future. Soon, in the mid-1960s, the Union Bank tower rose on the southeast shores of the Hill. Finally, as the 1960s ended, the remaining touchstones of Bunker Hill, the Castle and the Salt Box, were carted off to meet a fiery fate elsewhere, and with that, Bunker Hill was left to the developers.

Pick Up Your Cleaning
After demolition began in late 1961, businesses were instructed to relocate. Signs such as this one became increasingly common. This dry cleaners in the Selma (née Antlers) Hotel, at Fourth and Clay Streets, advises residents to pick up their clothing sooner rather than later. The Selma's demolition permit was issued in October 1962.

Elks Lodge
300 South Olive St.
▲ The Lodge Room for the Elks featured the Exalted Rulers Station at the end. The Loyal Order of Moose took over in 1925 and staged boxing matches in the auditorium.

After the Loyal Order of Moose vacated the building, it became the Royal dance hall, and a hotel for low-income tenants. A *Los Angeles Times* article about the demolition in Autumn 1962 described the "tattered remnants of the once-fancy curtain" hanging over its stage.

300 Block of Grand Avenue • Circa 1907
▲ From right, the Ryer, later known as the Alta Cresta and Stevens Apartments (Fred R. Dorn, 1904); the Kenneth (W.H. Mohr, 1905); and the Fleur-de-Lis, renamed the Capitol Hotel (Fred R. Dorn, 1903).

In Summer 1962, a Mercedes speeds past the demolition of the Kenneth, 325 South Grand Ave. The Capitol Hotel is already gone; the Stevens, at 321, stood until the end of 1964.

Essence of Sunshine and Noir

North on Grand Avenue • 1959
▲ From right: Colonial Flats, 312/316 South Grand Ave. and 308/310 South Grand Ave., a three-flat structure; Angels Flight Pharmacy; and the Lovejoy Apartments across Third Street.

At 310 South Grand Ave., demolition is underway in January 1963. Note that the crane sits on the site of the Colonial Flats.

Mission Apartments in 1919
▲ Looking north on Olive Street toward the Mission Apartments at Second Street.

The CRA-owned Mission in the hands of National House Wrecking Co. in Summer 1964. A County parking lot is north of Second Street; Olive Street ends at the new courthouse. Dorothy Chandler Pavilion opened that September.

160 Bunker Hill, Los Angeles

Third Street and Grand Avenue • June 1961

▲ 301/303, 305, and 311 South Grand Ave. 301/303 predates 1888, making it one of the oldest standing structures on the Hill; the other two were built between 1888 and 1894.

Demolition in March 1966 reveals the Castle and its neighbor 333 South Bunker Hill Ave. at left; 333 would be demolished in September 1966. Bunker Hill's first redevelopment project, the Union Bank Plaza, rises in the distance.

The View from the Palace Hotel
317 South Olive St. • Circa 1912

▲ From right to left, Elks Lodge, the six-bay pavilion of Angels Flight, Hotel Hillcrest, and the Astoria Apartments.

All the structures have been removed except Angels Flight by June 1965. The remaining buildings will go, too. Angels Flight will be put in storage, then rebuilt nearby in twenty-seven years.

Essence of Sunshine and Noir

Hotel Northern
420 West Second St.
Walter Jesse Saunders • 1913

By 1969, precious few structures remain. The Northern, once a first-class establishment, had lobbies fitted with Italian marble and mahogany paneling, featuring a Mission-style restaurant, and ladies' parlors in the French style.

Bunnie Burns had spent two months in the otherwise-vacated Northern. In 1964, she believed God had told her never to set foot outside the hotel again and to minister from her room. She was finally removed by multiple deputies and CRA representatives. June 4, 1969.

Last Stand of the Castle and the Salt Box

The Castle and Salt Box were saved from demolition in September 1968 by the Recreation and Parks Department, which donated land for Heritage Square, an open-air museum of Victorian Los Angeles. The houses moved to the new site in March 1969.

The Castle and Salt Box were to be the focal points of Heritage Square, slated to contain ornate houses, gas lamps, and horse-and-buggy traffic. The City neglected to protect the structures, and they were torched by vandals on October 9, 1969. And with that, the last of old Bunker Hill was gone.

Essence of Sunshine and Noir

A New Era

Bunker Hill contained all the ideals contemporary planners engineer into modern cities—walkability, density, mixed-use zoning. All this, replaced by an infrastructure that favored traffic separation, buildings turned inward from the street, and corporate plazas. A neighborhood was removed, its residents displaced and scattered, but in return we have a well-preserved collection of Modern, Late Modern and Postmodern architecture. In the 1980s, urban planners began to formulate a more pedestrian-friendly landscape. The redesign of the Civic Center Mall (which would become Grand Park) and other projects sought to maximize access and mobility, integrate the streetscape, add transit stops, and embed commercial activities. The evolution of post-redevelopment Bunker Hill may come at a cost, however. Ironically, as these newly iconic examples of modern architecture have come to signify Bunker Hill, they themselves have become concerns for preservationists. Much has been demolished or corrupted and much more is on the chopping block. The County Courthouse and Hall of Administration, for example, are more than sixty years old and threatened with demolition. Much of Bunker Hill, when undergoing its erasure in the early 1960s, was itself largely composed of sixty-year-old buildings.

Bunker Hill, Los Angeles

Mark Taper Forum
135 North Grand Ave.
Welton Becket & Associates • 1967
▲ The Mark Taper Forum is a drum-like building, covered in bas-relief by Jacques Overhoff. Its lobby features an abalone interior by famed stage designer Tony Duquette.

The Ahmanson Theatre
135 North Grand Ave.
Welton Becket & Associates • 1967
▶ The Ahmanson Theatre was once fronted by a wall of glass facing the plaza, its other sides faced with precast panels of tumbled-onyx aggregate. In 1994, the water feature was filled in and the Ahmanson was given a new façade minus the columns.

Becket's Memorial Pavilion Model
◀ Models and renderings of Memorial Pavilion by Welton Becket & Associates on display. Note the hanging lanterns in each bay of the pavilion, a feature that did not pass the planning stage. April 1961.

Essence of Sunshine and Noir

Civic Center Mall
Adrian Wilson & Associates,
Stanton & Stockwell,
Albert C. Martin & Associates;
landscape design by Cornell,
Bridgers & Troller • 1966

The view from Los Angeles City Hall, when nothing existed between the County Courthouse and Hall of Administration but parking and a dream. The idea for a half-mile Civic Center Mall was proposed in 1954 as part of a plan by Millard Sheets. January 1961.

Civic Center Mall broke ground in August 1963, and was officially named El Paseo de los Pobladores de Los Angeles in May 1964. Its most notable feature was the Arthur J. Will Memorial Fountain, a Space Age paraboloid shooting water into assorted pools. June 1976.

Bunker Hill Towers
800 West First St.
Robert E. Alexander & Associates
• 1969

Bunker Hill Towers broke ground in July 1967. The firm of Eckbo, Dean, Austin and Williams designed the landscape. Construction of two additional towers was canceled in the early 1970s, due to low occupancy in the existing buildings. 1972.

    From the promotional brochure: "Apartments are unusually spacious, allowing interesting furniture arrangements. You'll never feel cramped and will take pride in entertaining. Full-length windows frame exciting views of the city below."

Essence of Sunshine and Noir

World Trade Center
350 South Figueroa St.
Conrad Associates Architects • 1975

▲ The WTC is Los Angeles's business, cultural, and governmental core for international trade. Its lobby contains Tony Sheets's *History of World Commerce*, a 1000-foot-long concrete bas relief sculpture. The rooftop tennis club was designed by Langdon & Wilson.

Security Pacific Plaza
333 South Hope St.
Albert C. Martin & Associates • 1974

The fifty-five-story skyscraper is the only structure on the Hill aligned to the true north. The Alexander Calder sculpture *Four Arches* contrasts against the muted building, sheathed in granite from Pontevedra, Spain.

Angelus Plaza Retirement Housing
255 South Hill St.
Daniel Dworsky & Associates • 1980

◀ Grading began in early 1979 on a 4.2-acre, two-block site bordered by Hill, Second, Olive and Fourth Streets for Angelus Plaza, a federally subsidized residential development for senior citizens. It opened in May 1980.

Dworsky used modular precast concrete components in his design for Angelus Plaza. A ninety-year-old Moreton Bay Fig tree, the final living remnant of old Bunker Hill, was moved from the corner of Fourth and Hill to the courtyard of the complex in July 1981. By 1982, it housed 1,400 residents, the largest complex of its type in the United States.

Bonaventure Hotel
404 South Figueroa St.
John Portman • 1976
Portman's design includes five glass-skinned cylinders, rising from a two-story Brutalist concrete plaza. The hotel is distinguished by its ninety-foot interior atrium, housing the lobby, retail, and a large meandering lake. It is the Hill's first "mirror-building," with bronze glass to fully skin the structure.

Engstrum Hotel & Apartments
623 West Fifth St.
Robert Brown Young & Son
1912
The Engstrum, the last of the great Bunker Hill hotels, underwent sensitive restoration in the late 1970s. It was demolished in February 1986 for the Library Tower, as was Carleton Winslow's 1930 retaining wall. 1978.

Essence of Sunshine and Noir

Wells Fargo Bank
444 South Flower St.
Albert C. Martin & Associates • 1982
◀◀ The $110 million, forty-eight-story Wells Fargo Bank Tower opened September 1982 on the site of the former Sunkist Building. The tower features setbacks every eleven floors, with horizontal bands of stainless steel and reflective green glass.

Crocker Center
333 South Grand Ave.
Skidmore, Owings & Merrill • 1982
◀ Crocker Bank opened the first tower of its $300 million complex in July 1982, the second in July 1985. It was renamed Wells Fargo Center in November 1987. Its $20 million atrium was a 1.5-acre oasis of waterfalls, rare plants, and sculpture designed by Lawrence Halprin.

One California Plaza
300 South Grand Ave.
Arthur Erickson Architects • 1985
Museum of Contemporary Art (MOCA)
250 South Grand Ave.
Arata Isozaki • 1986
◀◀ The $1.2 billion California Plaza project initially called for three towers; One California Plaza broke ground October 1983. Two California Plaza (foundations at left) opened in 1992, but the third tower was never built, a victim of the 1990s financial downturn.

CRA law stipulates that 1.5% of a developer's budget go to public art; in the case of California Plaza, it built MOCA. MOCA is largely subterranean, clad in red sandstone and topped with pyramidal skylights.

Library Tower
623 West Fifth St.
Henry N. Cobb for I. M. Pei & Partners • 1990
◀ Developers Maguire Thomas received approval to build a super-tall Library Tower from City zoning authorities by purchasing potential development rights for the gutted-by-fire Central Library. The seventy-three-story tower is built with pale-grey Sardinian granite and composed of interlocking planes and curves, with an illuminated glass crown.

Bunker Hill, Los Angeles

The Grand
100 South Grand Ave.
Gehry Partners • *2021*

Construction began in 2019 on the thirty-nine-story residential tower and twenty-story hotel designed by Frank Gehry. It's part of the Grand Avenue Project which had funding from the City, County, New York's Related Companies, and the Chinese government.

AFTERWORD

People often ask, "What, if anything, is left of old Bunker Hill?" A handful of office buildings and a parking garage from the 1920s on the Hill's south end are about all that remain, but they don't exactly connote "Bunker Hill of yore." However, on the southwest corner of Olive and Fourth Streets, there's an old limestone retaining wall, the sole remnant of the 1902 Fremont Hotel. If Bunker Hill is our Acropolis, that ruin is our Parthenon. That wall should have a plaque—it should be landmarked—it is, instead, frequently defaced.

Where, then, does one go to have a vintage Hill experience, today? The premier destination would be Heritage Square, about two miles up the Pasadena Freeway from downtown, where Bunker Hill's Castle and Salt Box were moved in 1969. Despite the fact that those buildings were destroyed by arsonists, about a dozen other historic homes from around Los Angeles were transported onto museum property, including the Hale House, a grand Joseph Cather Newsom-designed structure worthy of Bunker Hill, and the Ford House that was formerly on Beaudry Street between First and Temple Streets, and the last surviving house built by the Beaudry brothers in existence. Another vintage adventure is a stroll around Angelino Heights, about a mile west of downtown near Echo Park, where the 1300 block of Carroll Avenue is particularly thick with restored Queen Anne homes. The South Bonnie Brae Tract Historic District and Alvarado Terrace Historic District, both in nearby Pico-Union, harbor some remarkable architectural monuments. The neighborhood of Highland Park, Los Angeles's largest Historic Preservation Overlay Zone, has both the hills and the vintage homes to help you believe you're in old Bunker Hill.

Another common question is what if the original houses on Bunker Hill remained and were not demolished and redeveloped? Perhaps the Hill could have been akin to New Orleans's French Quarter; after the Louisiana constitution officially designated New Orleans's Vieux Carré a historic district in 1936, the city guides began plugging New Orleans as "The City that Care Forgot" to the romantic delight of tourists ever since. In the postwar era, as plans to doom Bunker Hill were formulated, historic districts were designated in San Antonio, Texas; Alexandria and Williamsburg, Virginia; Winston-Salem, North Carolina, and Georgetown in Washington, D.C. In theory, rehabilitation could have made Bunker Hill a jewel. However, some writers and urbanists theorize that had Bunker Hill remained in place, when office space was required in the downtown area, mass redevelopment would have destroyed the historic Broadway theater district and great temples of finance along Spring Street. Moreover, while Bunker Hill was perhaps not the slum portrayed by government planners and media lackeys in the 1950s, it could have suffered along with the decline of downtown in the 1980s and '90s. It could have then undergone gentrification. The possibilities are endless, and endlessly fascinating.

Bunker Hill, rich palimpsest that it is, has been built anew and will be built anew again. Plans for construction of the city's tallest building—in fact, the tallest structure between Chicago and Hong Kong—were underway in 2020. The pavilion of Maxwell Starkman's 1983 Sheraton Grande Hotel, at 333 South Figueroa St., will be demolished to accommodate the 1,100-foot tower designed by DiMarzio Kato and developed by the Shenzhen New World Group. What may appear to us as a brave, new, futuristic Bunker Hill will one day be only a curious relic. One wonders what tomorrow's historians will make of Disney Hall and the Broad and Shenzhen tower; presupposing, of course, those structures have not already been replaced, in the great tradition of Bunker Hill.

IMAGE CREDITS

Agaman Collection # 62, 175
Andy Winn Collection # 5
Arizona State Library, Archives and Public Records, History and Archives Division # 60 (left)
Bison Archives # 27, 56 (top), 56 (middle), 56 (bottom), 57, 84, 91 (right), 94 (bottom), 154, 172
Bruce Wojcik Collection # 28 (right)
California State Library: California History Room # 25, 40, 58, 86 (bottom), 139 (top), 143 (bottom), 146, 147 (top), 147 (bottom), 150 (left); California History Room (courtesy of donor Arnold Hylen) # 96 (right), 102 (right), 104, 116 (bottom)
Christopher Rini Collection # 159 (top left)
CRA/LA # 38 (right), 42 (left), 42 (center), 110 (top left), 110 (top right), 111 (left), 111 (right), 113 (top left), 116 (top), 123 (bottom left)
The Cultural Landscape Foundation (copyright Charles A. Birnbaum) # 70 (right)
Getty Research Institute, Special Collections: Julius Shulman Photography Archive: Series IV (copyright J. Paul Getty Trust) # 44 (right), 66 (bottom)
Gordon Pattison # 8
History Colorado: Stephen H. Hart Research Center # 137 (top)
The Huntington Library, San Marino, California: Ernest Marquez Collection # 19, 93 (top right), 93 (bottom); Los Angeles Times Company Records # 138 (middle); Palmer Conner Collection of Color Slides of Los Angeles, 1950-1970 # 55 (right), 82 (right), 112 (top), 117 (left), 140 (top), 140 (bottom), 151, 153, 160 (top left), 160 (bottom right), 161 (top left), 161 (bottom left); Solano-Reeve Collection # 15 (left), 16; Southern California Edison Photographs and Negatives # 36, 149, 157; Theodore Seymour Hall Collection # 6 , 41, 97 (bottom), 108, 134 (left), 134 (right), 135, 155 (bottom right), 158, 159 (bottom right), 174, back cover
Jim Dawson Collection # 28 (left), 125
Johnson Archives # 14, 18, 22, 24, 46, 76, 88, 120, 128, 148 (top right), 167 (bottom)
Lara Swimmer Photography (copyright Lara Swimmer) # 73
Leo Politi Family # 43 (center), 118 (left)
Library of Congress # 53
Los Angeles County Museum of Art (LACMA) # 118 (right)
Los Angeles Public Library Photo Collection: Ansel Adams *Fortune* Magazine Collection # 105; George Mann Collection # 43 (right), 124; *Herald Examiner* Collection # 64 (left), 67, 83 (top), 124 (inset), 155 (left), 161 (bottom right), 163 (bottom); John & Mabel Haufe Collection # 110 (bottom); L. Mildred Harris Slide Collection # 70 (left); Security Pacific National Bank Collection # 26, 32 (left), 35, 78 (bottom left), 79 (top), 87, 90, 91 (left), 92 (bottom), 95, 96 (left), 97 (top), 100, 114, 115 (left), 117 (top right), 127 (bottom), 130, 143 (top), 150 (bottom right); *Valley Times* Collection # 113 (bottom)
Los Angeles Times # 142, 162 (top)
Metropolitan Museum of Art: Walker Evans Archive # 44 (left), 117 (bottom right), 159 (bottom left)
Natural History Museum of Los Angeles County: Seaver Center for Western History Research # 32 (right), 101 (bottom), 159 (top right)
Prelinger Archives # 152 (bottom)
Related Companies & Red Leaf # 171
UCLA Charles E. Young Research Library, Department of Special Collections # 31; Adelbert Bartlett Papers # 80 (bottom), 89, 92 (top); Allied Architects Association of Los Angeles Records # 50; Baruch Corporation Records # 148 (top left), 148 (bottom left); Lloyd Wright Papers (Collection 1561) # 52; *Los Angeles Daily News* Collection # 144; *Los Angeles Times* Photographic Archive # 138 (bottom); Photograph Album Collection # 78 (top left), 102 (top), 126, 136
University of California, Berkeley, Bancroft Library: Virgil Mirano Collection # 38 (left), 68 (left), 112 (bottom), 156 (left), 156 (top right), 163 (top)
USC Libraries Special Collections: "Dick" Whittington Photography Collection, 1924-1987 # 131, 132, 133 (left), 145 (top); California Historical Society Collection # 12, 37, 78 (right), 85, 99, 127 (top right), 129 (top right); *Los Angeles Examiner* Photographs Collection # 64 (right), 69 (bottom); Wayne Thom Photography Collection # 168 (top left), 170 (top right), 170 (bottom right)

▶▶ The view south on Clay Street. June 1957.

▶▶ The rummy, down on his luck, rifles through the detritus along Clay Street below the Angels Flight trestle. The Hill: haven for the destitute, the desolate, the damned. That's the story, anyway.

▼ A late night respite at Cooper Do-Nuts, 441 South Hill St. June 1959.

ACKNOWLEDGMENTS

In 2008, after three years of writing on Kim Cooper's "crime-a-day" Los Angeles history blog *1947project*, Kim suggested we focus on a place rather than a time. And so was born *OnBunkerHill.org*, where I wrote about historic Bunker Hill with crackerjack historians such as Christina Rice, Mary McCoy, and Joan Renner. I will forever be in their debt for helping hone my passion for the topic. Richard Schave has also been a tireless promoter of my work and a valued colleague. And of course Gordon Pattison, native son of Bunker Hill, has been an invaluable resource, whom I'm proud to call a friend.

Kim Cooper, Christopher Rini, and Timothy Doran were thoughtful, indispensable editors.

Generous thanks are due to Angel City Press publishers Paddy Calistro and Scott McAuley, and I am deeply grateful to Terri Accomazzo, tireless editor who saw this book through its many permutations, and J. Eric Lynxwiler, who designed it with such style, and Amy Inouye, who produced such a wonderful cover.

Christina Rice and Wendy Horowitz, of the Los Angeles Public Library Photo Collection, went above and beyond the call of duty, as did Erin Chase and Jennifer Watts at the Huntington Library. Gratitude is due to each of the many librarians I contacted for imaging requests, too numerous to list.

Special thanks go out to Jim Dawson, Marc Wanamaker, Richard Mechtly, Richard Wojcik, Bruce Wojcik, Chris Nichols, Paul Politi, Suzanne Politi Bischof, Carolyn Mirano, Rick Prelinger, and Susan Agaman.

And certainly, gratitude to all those who endured me holding forth about Bunker Hill at parties and in pubs. Most of all, enormous thanks to my ever-lovely, always-patient wife Nicole, who for these last ten years has put up with and encouraged me most of all.

LOCATION INDEX

Ahmanson Theatre, The, 66, 165
Almira Hershey Residence, 97
Albert Stephens House, 126
Alta Vista, 38–39, 61, 123
Alvarez & Moore, 60
Andrew Wilson Potts House, 79
Angels Flight, 8, 26, 28–29, 38–39, 56, 60, 69, 74, 126, 129, 139, 161, 174–175
Angels Flight Café, 64, 152
Angels Flight Pharmacy, 9, 160
Angels Rest, 28
Angelus Plaza Retirement Housing, 168
Argyle, 98
Astoria Apartments, 123, 161
Auditorium Hotel, The, 148
Avalon Apartments, 151
B.P.O.E. Temple, Lodge No. 99, 114
Berke Mansion, 86
Bernhard Sens/Dr. James Green House, 112
Bishop Apartments, 111
Bixby House, 18
Black Building, 129, 132, 134
Bob's Café, 120, 125
Bonaventure Hotel, 169
Boswell, The, 120
Bradbury Mansion, 18, 57, 154
Brousseau Mansion, 82
Brunson Mansion, 12, 37
Bryan Residence, 32
Buena Vista Tavern, 46
Bunker Hill Playground and Recreation Center, 111
Bunker Hill Towers, 71, 167
California Plaza, 71–72, 170
Carleton, 7, 102, 169
Castle Towers, 65, 97
Castle, The, 12, 91, 163
Hotel Cecil, The, 55
Central Library, 7, 52, 170
Chestmere Apartments, 57
Cinderella's, 134
Civic Center Mall, 164, 166
Colonial Flats, 101–102, 160
Congregation Beth Israel, 113
Cooper Do-Nuts, 174
Court Flight, 29, 139
Cowper Homestead Property, 129
Crocker Center, 170
Crocker Citizens Bank Tower, 70
Department of Water and Power, 9, 65–66
Divine Order of the Royal Arms of the Great Eleven, 117
Dr. Johann Carl Zahn House, 83
Dr. Joseph Pomeroy Widney House, 78
Earlcliff, 102

Eddy Park, 28
Elks Lodge, 69, 159, 161
Ems, 36, 106
Engstrum Hotel & Apartments, 169
Federation of Jewish Welfare Organizations, 150
Fleur-de-lis, 32, 37, 159
Fort Moore Pioneer Memorial, 48
Fort Street Methodist Episcopal Church, 12
Frank Walker House, 80
Fremont Hotel, 56, 65, 106, 155, 173
George H. Stewart House, 92
George Hugh Smith House, 93
George M. Holton House, 82
Gibson Apartments, 55
Granada, 107
Grand Central Garage, 145
Grand, The, 145, 171
Hall of Administration, The, 65–66, 72, 141, 164, 166
Harley Taft House, 76
Harry Chandler House, 138
Herman F. Baer House, 93
Hildreth Mansion, 65, 96, 110, 116
Hill Cemetery, 136
Hill Street Tunnel, 46, 57, 140
Hillcrest, The, 69
Hopecrest, 110
Hotel Broadway, 29
Hotel Clark Garage, The, 144
Hotel Clayton, 59
Hotel El Moro, 126
Hotel Lincoln, 127
Hotel Munn, 33
Hotel Northern, 162
Howard M. Sale House, 126
Jesus Manzo Adobe, 77
John Alexander Wills Mansion, 87
Judge Anson Brunson Mansion, 94
Lady McDonald Residence, 93
Leonard Rose Mansion, 92
Lewis Leonard Bradbury Mansion, 88
Library Tower, 169–170
Llewellyn Bixby House, 80
Locke House, 126
Los Angeles Public High School, 138
Lovejoy, The, 124, 160
Lux Theater, 113
Majestic, 103
Marcella, 105
Margaret Crocker Mansion, 85
Mark Taper Forum, 66, 165
Masonic Temple, 127
Melrose, 8, 35, 65, 100–101, 156
Melrose Annex, 101

Melrose Hotel, The, 11, 35, 65
Mills House, 36
Milo S. Baker House, 94
Minnewaska/Dome, 107
Mission Apartments, 106, 160
Monarch Hotel, 70, 150
Moore Cliff, 126
Music Center, 9, 63, 65–66, 72
Norfolk Apartments, 110
Nugent, 9, 102, 116
Olive Street School, 115
One California Plaza, 170
Pacific Electric Subway Terminal Building, 143
Pacific Electric Train Depot, 143
Pacific Telephone Complex, 153
Palace Hotel, 161
People's National Bank, 146
Pierre Larronde House, 94
Queen Apartments, 48, 105
Reverend Edward Hildreth Mansion, 96
Richelieu, The, 155
Robert M. Widney House, 78–79
Rose Mansion, 12, 22
Salt Box, 8, 80, 91, 158, 163, 173
Savoy Auto Park, The, 145
Second Street Tunnel, 98, 143
Security Pacific Plaza, 168
Sherwood Apartments, 156
Sons of the Revolution Headquarters and Library, 113
Southern California Edison Building, The, 149
St. Angelo, 98
State Mutual Building and Loan Association, 147
Sunkist Building, 150, 170
Sunshine Apartments, 118
Taft Duplex, 78
Temple and Workman Bank, 18
Temple Baptist Auditorium, 148
Title Guarantee and Trust Company, 147
Touraine Apartments, 30
Union Bank Square, 70
University Club, 129, 134
Vegetarian Café, The, 129
Walt Disney Concert Hall, 71–72
Wells Fargo Bank, 170
Westmoreland Place, 32
William W. Widney House, 79
World Trade Center, 72, 168
Wright and Callender Building, 132
Young Women's Christian Association, 132